KRISTALLNACHT

The Nazi Terror That Began the Holocaust

The Holocaust Through Primary Sources

James M. Deem

Enslow Publishers, Inc.
40 Industrial Road
Box 398
Berkeley Heights, NJ 07922
USA

http://www.enslow.com

Library of Congress Cataloging-in-Publication Data

Deem, James M.

Kristallnacht : the Nazi terror that began the Holocaust / James M. Deem.

p. cm. — (The Holocaust through primary sources)

Includes bibliographical references and index.

Summary: "Discusses Kristallnacht, a four-day pogrom instigated by the Nazis against Germany's Jews, including stories from the victims, witnesses and perpetrators of the attack, and how it marked the beginning of the Holocaust"—Provided by publisher.

ISBN 978-0-7660-3324-5

1. Jews—Persecutions—Germany—Juvenile literature. 2. Kristallnacht, 1938—Juvenile literature. I. Title.

DS134.255.D44 2011

940.53'1842—dc22

2010015696

Paperback ISBN 978-1-59845-345-4

Printed in China

052011 Leo Paper Group, Heshan City, Guangdong, China

10 9 8 7 6 5 4 3 2 1

To Our Readers: We have done our best to make sure all Internet Addresses in this book were active and appropriate when we went to press. However, the author and the publisher have no control over and assume no liability for the material available on those Internet sites or on other Web sites they may link to. Any comments or suggestions can be sent by e-mail to comments@enslow.com or to the address on the back cover.

Every effort has been made to locate all copyright holders of material used in this book. If any errors or omissions have occurred, please contact us at www.enslow.com. We will try to make corrections in future editions.

For text permission credit lines, please see p. 124.

Illustration Credits: Associated Press, p. 110; Bildarchiv Preussischer Kulturbesitz / Art Resource, NY, p. 49; Enslow Publishers, Inc., p. 14; Courtesy of Ernest Foulkes, p. 107; © Hans Asemissen / akg-images / The Image Works, p. 58; Courtesy of Jurgen Herbst, p. 75; © Knorr + Hirth / Sueddeutsche Zeitung Photo / The Image Works, p. 23; © Mary Evans Picture Library / The Image Works, pp. 32, 94; © Military and Historical Image Bank, p. 81; © National Maritime Museum, London / The Image Works, p. 109; © Scherl / Sueddeutsche Zeitung Photo / The Image Works, p. 46; © Sueddeutsche Zeitung Photo / The Image Works, p. 101; ullstein bild / The Granger Collection, New York, p. 89; USHMM, pp. 15, 25, 39, 67, 79, 111; USHMM courtesy of Bildarchiv der Oesterreichische, p. 99; USHMM, courtesy of Bildarchiv Preussischer Kulturbesitz, pp. 5, 77; USHMM, courtesy of Dana Upton, p. 93; USHMM, courtesy of Dr. Adolf Vees, p. 43; USHMM, courtesy of Edgar and Hana Krasa, p. 71; USHMM, courtesy of Harold Royall, p. 95; USHMM, courtesy of Henry Schwarzbaum, p. 65; USHMM, courtesy of Henry Straus, p. 105; USHMM, courtesy of Jewish Community of Giessen, p. 59; USHMM, courtesy of Lev Sviridov, p. 56; USHMM, courtesy of Margaret Chelnick, p. 41; USHMM, courtesy of Michael Irving Ashe, p. 21; USHMM, courtesy of Morris Rosen, p. 19; USHMM, courtesy of National Archives and Records Administration, pp. 7, 30, 35, 98; USHMM, courtesy of Ralph Harpuder, p. 112; USHMM, courtesy of Richard Freimark, p. 28; USHMM, courtesy of Ruth Herz Goldschmidt, p. 51; USHMM, courtesy of Virginius Dabney, p. 11; USHMM, courtesy of William O. McWorkman, p. 84; USHMM, courtesy of YIVO Institute for Jewish Research, New York, p. 68; Yad Vashem Photo Archives, p. 63.

Cover Illustration: Yad Vashem Photo Archives (Jewish men arrested in Baden-Baden, Germany, during Kristallnacht); USHMM, courtesy of Fritz Gluckstein (Star of David artifact).

Contents

INTRODUCTION

In the very early morning hours of November 10, 1938, twelve-year-old Francis Schott and his sister were asleep in their family's apartment in Solingen, Germany. Suddenly, they were awakened by the sound of their front door splintering into pieces. From their bedroom, the startled children could hear men speaking in loud voices. The men did not seem to be robbers for they were destroying as much as they could. Over and over again, Francis and his sister heard the sound of shattering glass.

Soon their mother slipped into their bedroom and shut the door behind her. Francis did not dare ask her what was happening, but he sensed that the intruders were Nazis who had "come to get us."[1] The Schotts, like other German Jews, had been subjected to terrible humiliations and persecutions since Adolf Hitler and his National Socialist Party (the Nazis, for short) had begun to run the country. Their father, a well-respected doctor and hospital administrator, had been fired from his job because of Nazi decrees that prohibited Jews from working as physicians.

When the men left, the family inspected the apartment. Their father's cello and their prized piano had been hacked to pieces. Their mother's china and crystal had been smashed on the floor. The living quarters were ruined.

Francis knew that this night—which has come to be known as *Kristallnacht*, or the Night of Broken Glass—signaled the end of the world as he knew it and the beginning of a terrible new one. That night, he learned that the "orderly world in which only the police can get you and won't come unless you are a criminal . . . is gone. By fanning prejudice into hate, a government can turn a populace into assault troops."[2]

Warning Signs

Schott and his family were far from alone that night, as the Nazis targeted Germany's Jews, their homes, their businesses, and their synagogues. But Kristallnacht had not happened without warning.

A group of Nazis broke into Francis Schott's home and destroyed the apartment. This is a private Jewish home in Vienna, Austria, that was vandalized during Kristallnacht.

Hitler and the Nazis had made it clear during the five years and nine months that they had been in power that Germany was to be populated with an "Aryan master race," a term that the Nazis used to mean "pure-blooded German." The Nazis believed that Jews—and many other groups, including the Sinti and Roma (sometimes called "Gypsies"), Jehovah's Witnesses, homosexuals, and physically and mentally disabled individuals—were inferior to "Aryans."

At the time, less than 1 percent of the German population was Jewish.[3] But this did not matter to Hitler and his Nazi followers, who wanted to rid Germany of the "Jewish race" and make the country *Judenfrei* (that is, "Free from Jews").

Appointed chancellor on January 30, 1933, Hitler wasted no time in declaring Germany's Jews as "un-German." On April 1, 1933, the Nazi Party staged a boycott of Jewish businesses and professionals, such as lawyers and doctors. Flyers listing the targeted businesses were posted in public places, and members of the Nazi SA (Hitler's storm troopers) were stationed outside many Jewish stores, trying to prevent Germans from entering. Some SA carried signs that read, "Don't buy from Jews!"[4]

Six days after the boycott, a law was enacted that prohibited Jewish teachers, professors, and civil servants from working; all teachers were required to be members of the Nazi Party. New decrees required Jewish-owned shops to display the six-pointed Star of David (a symbol of Judaism) and the German word *Jude* (Jew) on their front windows to discourage Germans from shopping there.

A Nazi SA member stands outside a Jewish department store on April 1, 1933, during the Nazi boycott of Jewish businesses and professionals. The sign hanging outside the store reads: "Germans defend yourselves; don't buy from Jews!"

Against the Law

During Hitler's first three years as chancellor, his government approved numerous laws that prohibited many German Jews from working, enjoying their rights as German citizens, and receiving an education. Among the worst were the Nuremberg Laws, instituted by the Nazis on September 15, 1935. These two laws clearly spelled out the terms of German citizenship (Jews could not be citizens) and German marriage (Jews and Germans could not marry).

The overall purpose of these ever-restrictive laws was to make life so difficult for German Jews that they would emigrate to other countries. By 1938, some 250,000 Jews had left Germany, the largest portion of them (155,000) going to the United States.[5] Although some Jews wished to remain in Germany, believing that the hatred would eventually pass, others would have gladly left, but countries were no longer willing to give them visas.

Convinced that the world did not care about the fate of the Jews, the Nazis took even more drastic measures. This included the deportation of 17,000 Jews of Polish descent who had been living in Germany for many years. Near the end of October 1938, they were rounded up and sent on special train cars to the Polish border. No one was allowed to take more than one suitcase and a small amount of money (ten marks). At the border, eight thousand people were not permitted entry into Poland or reentry into Germany. They would be held in refugee camps in Zbaszyn, Poland, for almost a year.

The Assassination of a Diplomat

Among these detainees was the Grynszpan family, Polish Jews who had settled in Hanover, Germany. One of their children, Herschel, was living in Paris illegally with his aunt and uncle. Herschel's father, mother, his sister Esther, and his brother Marcus, however, were among those deported to Poland.

Esther wrote to Herschel, telling him what had happened. When he received the postcard on November 3, he was incensed. He was also in trouble; his attempts to become a legal resident in France had failed, and now, if he were caught by the police, he would be sent to Poland as well. He told his uncle that he was not willing to go to Poland, reportedly saying, "I'd rather die like a dog."[6]

On November 7, he purchased a revolver. Then he went to the German Embassy in Paris and shot Ernst vom Rath, an embassy official, as a statement of his anger and frustration. Herschel made no attempt to run and was seized by embassy staff and then arrested by the French police.

When the assassination attempt on vom Rath was announced, the Nazis went to work creating propaganda-filled news for German newspapers and radio stations. By supplying propaganda (information that omitted certain facts and added outright lies), the Nazis wanted to encourage German citizens to share their political beliefs; this was a technique that Hitler's government had perfected.

Four hours after the crime, the Nazi government released its first news report to the German media under the headline: "Impudent Jewish Attack in the German Embassy in Paris."[7] Later that evening, other accounts indicated that Grynszpan was encouraged to assassinate vom Rath by international Jewish organizations that wished to eliminate the Nazi Party.[8] The Nazis wished to convey one message: All Jews were responsible for the shooting of vom Rath.

In Grynszpan's act and the resulting propaganda, the excuse for increased violence against Jews—Kristallnacht—was born.

Kristallnacht: November 7–10

Although many historians have focused on the events that occurred on November 9 and 10, 1938, Kristallnacht was not a twenty-four-hour event. Rather, it was a four-day *pogrom* (a brutal and violent action) against the Jews of Germany.

It began with a series of "local anti-Jewish riots" in smaller towns.[9] The first rioting occurred late in the evening on November 7, in Kassel, a city in north central Germany. Started by a local Nazi official, the riot began when a thousand-person mob, mostly made up of SA and SS troops, broke into and destroyed a Jewish restaurant, then a synagogue, and then some twenty Jewish businesses.[10] Five other towns near Kassel were also the scene of such violence that night.

The next morning, as vom Rath lingered between life and death in a Paris hospital, headlines in the Nazi-controlled German press played up the antisemitism. One headline read:

After Herschel Grynszpan assassinated Ernst vom Rath, the Nazis quickly put out propaganda blaming all Jews for the German official's death. This is the front page of the Nazi publication *Der Stürmer* with a caricature of Grynszpan crucifying vom Rath. The headline describes the assassination as part of a larger plot by world Jewry to slaughter the German people.

JEWISH MURDER ATTEMPTED IN PARIS—MEMBER OF THE GERMAN EMBASSY CRITICALLY WOUNDED BY SHOTS— THE MURDERING KNAVE A 17-YEAR-OLD JEW.[11]

Although Jewish newspapers would have responded to the propaganda, Nazi officials had stopped their publication that day.

That night, further riots, instigated by local and regional Nazi officials, took place in over twenty-four towns in the German state of Hesse.[12] These did not stop until the early morning of November 9.

The November Pogrom

Late in the afternoon on November 9, Ernst vom Rath died. Nazi leaders had anticipated his death and were ready to organize a national pogrom that built on the local riots that had occurred the last two days.

By the early evening of November 9, Hitler had learned of the death while attending a large reception of Nazi leaders in Munich, the symbolic birthplace of the Nazi Party. Hitler turned to Joseph Goebbels, his minister for propaganda and public enlightenment, and told him that the Nazis should not organize any riots or demonstrations against Jews. However, if they occurred, the Nazis should not stop them. Hitler then left the reception, effectively turning over the pogrom to Goebbels, who was known for his violent hatred of Jews.

That night, Goebbels gave the closing speech at the reception. His message was clear: The Nazis were "not to appear to the outside as the originator of the demonstrations," but they were to "organize and carry them out."[13] When his speech was finished, party members rushed to telephones to call their offices around Germany, alerting their members about the pogrom. One witness described how Kristallnacht began in Emden, Germany:

> Dead silence—not a sound to be heard in the town. The lamps in the street, the lights in the shops and in the houses are out. It is 3:30 a.m. All of a sudden noises in the street break into my sleep, a wild medley of shouts and shrieks. I listen, frightened and alarmed, until I distinguish words: Get out, Jews! Death to the Jews![14]

David H. Buffum, the American consul in Leipzig, Germany, filed a report on the events of Kristallnacht in his city. It began about 3:00 A.M.:

> In one of the Jewish [neighborhoods] an eighteen year old boy was hurled from a three story window to land with both legs broken on a street littered with burning beds and other household furniture and effects from his family's and other apartments. . . . Three synagogues in Leipzig were fired simultaneously by incendiary bombs and all sacred objects and records desecrated or destroyed, in most instances hurled through the windows and burned in the streets. . . .[15]

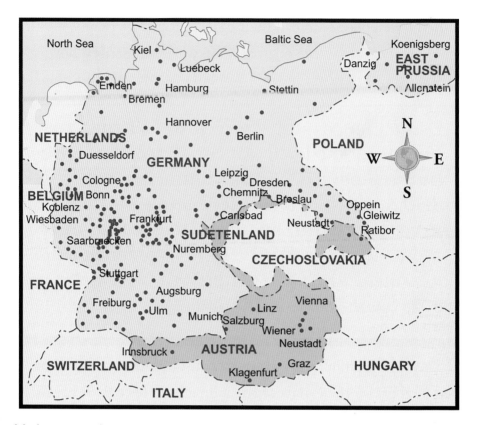

Violent attacks against Jews and their property took place all over Germany and annexed German territory. This map shows many cities where synagogues were destroyed during Kristallnacht.

During the four-day pogrom, the participants were mostly Nazi SAs as well as German citizens (workers, neighbors, and even some schoolchildren). Although "there is no question that most Germans were *not* directly involved" in the violent pogrom, many either watched the destruction or quickly learned about it.[16] What's more, many thousands of Germans—including a very large proportion of women—participated in the plunder of Jewish-owned property from businesses and homes.

The Aftermath of Kristallnacht

By the time it was over on the morning of November 11, 7,500 Jewish businesses and 275 synagogues had been destroyed or burned. No records, however, were kept on the number of Jewish homes or apartments that were vandalized during the pogrom.

But Kristallnacht was not only about the destruction of property. It was also about the destruction of people. Initially, the Nazis reported thirty-six Jews had been killed, but this figure was raised to ninety-one a few months later. A closer look revealed that some 236 people died, including 43 women and 13 children.[17] Some were killed defending their homes or businesses, some were hideously abused and died from their injuries, and

Residents watch the burning of the ceremonial hall at a Jewish cemetery in Graz, Austria.

some committed suicide.[18] But no figures were kept on the number of Jews who survived after being beaten during the pogrom.

In addition, 30,000 Jewish men and teenagers between the ages of sixteen and sixty—about 10 percent of the entire Jewish community then in Germany—had been arrested and shipped to one of three concentration camps: Sachsenhausen (near Berlin), Buchenwald (near Erfurt), and Dachau (near Munich).[19] There, they were degraded, abused, tortured, and sometimes murdered by Nazi guards. The surviving prisoners were released over a period of five or six months. In all, historians have estimated that over five thousand Jews died in the three concentration camps.[20]

After the violence ended, the persecution continued when even stricter laws were enacted: Jewish children were now prohibited from attending German schools, permitted only to attend segregated schools; Jews could no longer drive or own cars; Jews were required to close their businesses or sell them to Aryans at reduced prices; Jews could no longer attend any public events such as concerts, movies, or fairs.

As for the cost of repairing Germany after the destruction of Kristallnacht, Nazi leaders decided that Jews would not be allowed to have their damages covered by insurance companies; they had to pay for repairs themselves. A fine of one billion marks was to be divided among the Jews in Germany. It would be, as Hermann Göring, a high-ranking Nazi announced, "a punishment for their abominable crimes."[21] This fine was the "equivalent of one-sixth of all the property owned by Jews in Germany."[22]

The Coming Holocaust

After Kristallnacht, most Jews wished to leave Germany as quickly as possible, but obtaining a visa from another country was very difficult. A few days after Kristallnacht, for example, Switzerland stopped the entry of almost all Jews. Other countries, including the United States, held fast to the quotas they had already established, unwilling to increase them.

Visas generally were granted only when a person could offer proof of adequate financial means. With the enormous fine penalizing Jews for the destruction of Kristallnacht and new laws prohibiting many Jews from working, many were unable to prove that they had enough money to obtain a visa, even if one were available.

Hitler mocked the countries that were unwilling to help the Jews. In a speech to the German parliament on January 30, 1939, he said that although "the whole democratic world is oozing sympathy for the poor tormented Jewish people," it "remains hard-hearted and obdurate when it comes to helping them."[23] Then he offered an obvious warning about what he had in mind if a world war would begin; it could only lead to "the annihilation of the Jewish race in Europe!"[24]

Time was running out for the Jews of Germany. In less than a year, on September 1, 1939, Germany would invade Poland, starting World War II. Germany's borders would be closed, and emigration would no longer be possible, trapping all remaining Jews.

Clearly, Kristallnacht was the opening movement of what would soon become the Holocaust in Nazi-controlled Europe.

1 Herschel Grynszpan

Herschel Grynszpan received the terrible news from his sister Esther by postcard on November 3, 1938. A police officer had knocked at the Grynszpan family's door in Hanover, Germany, on Thursday night, October 27, and told them to go immediately to police headquarters. There, they saw many other people from their neighborhood—all of them Polish Jews, who had settled in Germany long ago.

As Esther wrote in her postcard:

> We were not told what it was all about, but we saw that everything was finished for us. Each of us had an extradition order pressed into his hand, and one had to leave Germany before the 29th. . . . I asked . . . to go home to get at least a few things. I went, accompanied by a [police officer], and packed the necessary clothes in a suitcase. And that is all I saved. We don't have a "Pfennig."[1]

Herschel was devastated by the news that his family and as many as 17,000 other Polish Jews were being deported to Poland, the first large transport intended to rid Germany of all its Jews.

Herschel wrote back, but there was little that he could do. He folded the postcard and put it in his wallet. He was about to make a life-changing and world-affecting decision.

Growing up in Germany

Herschel had grown up in Hanover. His parents, Sendel and Ryfka, had both been born in an area of Russia that had once been Poland. They obtained Polish citizenship at the end of World War I when Poland became independent from Russian rule. Although they moved to Germany, each member of the Grynszpan family held a Polish passport.

At the age of fourteen, Herschel dropped out of public school. Although many of his teachers acknowledged his intelligence, he had been viewed as "lazy."[2] He tried enrolling in a five-year program at a yeshiva (a religious school for Jews), but he lasted only eleven months. He attempted to find

This photo of Herschel Grynszpan was taken after his arrest by French authorities.

work, but because he was an orthodox Jew and could not work on Saturdays (as required by his religious beliefs), he was unable to find a job.

In the end, a man at his synagogue advised him to leave Germany. As Herschel recalled, the man told him, "A boy like you can't stay here under such conditions. In Germany, a Jew is not a man, but is treated like a dog."[3] The man suggested that Herschel go to France. His father's brother, Abraham, lived in Paris. When Herschel's father wrote Abraham, he agreed to let Herschel stay with him and his wife.

Living in Paris

Once Herschel arrived in Paris, he faced trouble with French and German authorities because he had entered France illegally. Both his Polish passport and German reentry visa were due to expire, and French authorities refused to give him a residency permit. He was notified that he would be expelled from the country as of August 15, 1938.[4] This order also endangered his uncle and aunt, for if Herschel continued to stay with them after the date of expulsion, they could face arrest.

He had few options. Because he held a Polish passport, he could travel to Poland, a country that was not his home. He could join the French Foreign Legion. In despair, he also considered killing himself.[5] As the deadline approached, his uncle and aunt moved to another apartment nearby, leaving Herschel alone. Although French police searched their new home for Herschel, they did not know that he remained in the old apartment.

This was the situation that Herschel found himself in when he read that Germany was sending Jews with Polish passports back to Poland. He wondered if his family had been selected. Then he received his sister's postcard.

Herschel was furious. "Again and again I asked myself, 'What have [Jews] done to deserve such a fate?' And I couldn't find any answer to the question."[6]

A view of Zbaszyn, the site of a refugee camp for Jews of Polish descent who were deported from Germany. Grynszpan's family was among the 17,000 Jews expelled to the Polish border town.

November 7, 1938

A few days later, Herschel asked his uncle to send money to his family. After all, his father had sent Abraham a generous sum to help care for Herschel. Now Herschel wanted Abraham to help his family survive in Poland.

Uncle Abraham preferred to wait for more news before he would agree to send any money. This angered Herschel so much that he stormed out of the apartment. That night, he wandered the streets of Paris and came across a gun shop displaying revolvers in the front window. Rather than go back to his uncle's apartment, he rented a hotel room. He described that night:

> I went to bed, but I did not sleep well because of the bad dreams I had. I saw myself going into the gun shop. I also had visions of my family's plight. I woke up three times during the night. Each time my heart was beating fast. To make it calm down, I put my hand on my chest.[7]

The next morning, he bought a revolver, loaded it with bullets, and went to the German Embassy in Paris. He told the staff that he had important documents for the ambassador and was shown to the office of the official in charge that morning: Ernst vom Rath.

When vom Rath asked for the mysterious documents, Herschel said, "You're a filthy German, and in the name of [the deported Polish] Jews, here is the document!"[8] He drew his gun, its price tag still dangling from the trigger-guard, and shot five times. Two bullets hit the stunned vom Rath. Embassy staff rushed in; some attended to the

Ernst vom Rath

wounded diplomat, while others held Herschel, who did not resist. A French police officer stationed outside arrested Herschel and took him to the nearest headquarters.

When he was searched by police, they found an unsent postcard that Herschel had written before he had bought the gun. It read:

> My dear parents. I could not do otherwise. May God forgive me. My heart bleeds at the news of [the] Jews' suffering. I must protest in such a way that the world will hear me. I must do it. Forgive me. Herschel.[9]

An Unknown Ending

Adolf Hitler sent his personal doctors to Paris, but they could not save vom Rath, and he died late in the afternoon of November 9. As Kristallnacht unfolded, Herschel Grynszpan remained in a French jail. His arrest by French police prevented him from being taken away by German officials to Germany where a certain death most likely awaited him. Instead, French officials imprisoned him while he awaited trial.

When Germany invaded France in 1940, Nazi authorities began searching for Grynszpan's location. Once he was found, he was sent to Germany and eventually imprisoned in the Sachsenhausen concentration camp. Although there is no firm evidence, some suspect that he was later transferred to the Magdeburg sub-camp of Buchenwald. When the guards came to take him away, he reportedly told another prisoner, "Don't think that I am afraid. When I reach the end I will spit three times on this sinister band of rogues."[10]

That transfer, if it occurred, took place in late September 1942. Herschel Grynszpan was never heard from again. Family members who survived the war searched for him and worked to uncover the details of his disappearance. His family and his original lawyer believed he had died at Sachsenhausen. Finally, in 1960, the West German government concluded that he had died. Although they did not know when, they gave him an official date of death: May 8, 1945—otherwise known as VE (or Victory in Europe) Day, the date that World War II officially ended.[11]

The front page of the German newspaper *Münchner Neueste Nachrichten* featured an article entitled "Jewish Murder Attack in the German Embassy" on November 8, 1938, the day after Grynszpan shot vom Rath.

WHAT HAPPENED TO THE GRYNSZPANS

Herschel's parents, Sendel and Ryfka, as well as his brother and sister, survived the war by escaping to Russia. His parents eventually moved to Israel. Sendel testified at the trial of Adolf Eichmann, a notorious Nazi who was captured in Argentina after the war. During his testimony, Sendel described what had happened during the Nazi deportation of the Polish Jews in October 1938:

> When we reached the border, we were searched to see if anybody had any money, and anybody who had more than ten marks, the balance was taken from him. . . . We walked two kilometers on foot to the Polish border. They told us to go—the SS men were whipping us, those who lingered they hit, and blood was flowing on the road. They tore away their little baggage from them, they treated us in a most barbaric fashion. . . . They shouted at us, "Run! Run!" I myself received a blow and I fell in the ditch. My son helped me, and he said "Run, run dad—otherwise you'll die."[12]

Many people, including several survivors of concentration camps, testified against Eichmann. He was found guilty and hanged on May 31, 1962.

As for Herschel's uncle and aunt who had cared for him in Paris, they were arrested by French police shortly after vom Rath's assassination for harboring an illegal immigrant; they were tried and found guilty. After serving a month of their sentences, they were quietly released. When Germany invaded France, they were detained as Jews. Herschel's aunt was taken to a farm near the Spanish border where she worked until the end of the war. His uncle was placed on a transport to Auschwitz, a death camp, where he died.[13]

2 Joseph Goebbels

The Nazi mastermind behind the national Kristallnacht was Joseph Goebbels, Hitler's minister of propaganda and public enlightenment. Although Goebbels was an early supporter of the Nazi Party, he fell far short of the Nazi ideal of the "Aryan."

Raised in a devout Catholic family, Goebbels was diagnosed with polio when he was four years old. As he grew older, this illness left him with a limp and affected his growth. As one biographer explained: "He was very slight in build and his shoulders sloped steeply. He was little more than five feet tall and his weight was in the region of one hundred pounds. He walked with an unmistakable limp, but had become adept at disguising it. . . ."[1]

His family was not well off financially, but they recognized how intelligent he was and made sacrifices that allowed him to attain a higher education. In 1921, he graduated with a doctorate from Heidelberg University. His favorite professor at Heidelberg was the noted poet Friedrich Gundolf, who was Jewish. Goebbels also had a serious Jewish girlfriend named Else; they planned to get married. But Goebbels was about to develop a virulent antisemitism.

Becoming a Nazi

Hoping to support himself as a writer, Goebbels sent off his manuscripts to different publishers, but his writing was rejected. One rejection from the Ullstein Press, among the largest and most respected publishing companies in Germany, troubled Goebbels greatly. A Jewish family owned the company, and Goebbels became convinced that his work had not been given a chance; he began to blame the Jews for this rejection.

Around the same time, Goebbels heard Hitler speak and became interested in the political views of the Nazis. In 1925,

Adolf Hitler (right) and Joseph Goebbels (left) share a meal together. Hitler began to notice Goebbels's speaking abilities, and the two men began to meet more often.

he was hired as an editorial assistant for a weekly Nazi newspaper and began to give pro-Nazi speeches in Berlin to recruit more party members. Late that same year, he met Hitler for the first time. During this time, Goebbels and Else tried to continue their romance, but, in 1926, she finally ended their relationship. Goebbels wrote about the event in his diary, which he kept almost daily from 1923 to 1945: "Else sent me a brief and frightfully matter-of-fact letter breaking it all off. What am I to do? She is, of course, completely right. We can no longer even be comrades to one another. Between us there is a whole world."[2]

Momentarily hurt, Goebbels went on with his life, making a name for himself for his Nazi propaganda and for his speeches. Hitler began to notice his abilities, and the two met and spoke on a number of occasions. Goebbels's diaries describe these meetings, especially one on November 23, 1926:

> My joy is great. [Hitler] greets me like an old friend. He speaks to us all the evening. I can't hear enough of it. He gives me his picture . . . inscribed "Heil Hitler!". . . I would love to have Hitler as my friend. His picture stands on my table. I could not bear to have to doubt that man![3]

Hitler was also impressed with Goebbels and asked him to speak at rallies all around the country. After Goebbels gave a speech in Munich, Hitler visited with him. Goebbels wrote about that moment: "Hitler hugs me. My eyes are full of tears. I am happier than ever in my life."[4]

In Goebbels, Hitler had found a man with two important attributes, as Hitler explained: "intelligence and the gift of oratory."[5] As a result, he named Goebbels to be the head of party propaganda. In this position, he learned to master the use of propaganda to sway people toward the beliefs of Nazism.

When Hitler was appointed chancellor in 1933, he selected Goebbels as minister for propaganda and public enlightenment. Within a month, Goebbels had organized his first event: the

A member of the SA throws "un-German" books into a bonfire in Berlin, Germany, on May 10, 1933.

boycott of Jewish businesses on April 1, 1933. A month later, he permitted the German Students' Association to hold a public book burning, primarily in Berlin, as well as in towns with universities. Books to be destroyed comprised those by Jewish authors (including works by his favorite professor) and books that opposed Nazi policies and politics. Some twenty thousand books were burned at dusk in Berlin. Then Goebbels spoke to the crowd and proclaimed the book burning "a strong, great, and symbolic act" against "the evil spirit of the past."[6]

Sir Nevile Henderson, the British ambassador to Germany from 1931 to 1939, got to know Goebbels during this period; he wrote that Goebbels

> . . . was probably the most intelligent, from a purely brain point of view, of all the Nazi leaders. He never speechified; he always saw and stuck to the point; he was an able debater and, in private conversation, astonishingly fair-minded and reasonable. . . . When, however, he was on a public platform or had a pen in his hand . . . no lie was too blatant for him.[7]

Kristallnacht

When Herschel Grynszpan shot Ernst vom Rath, the local riots on November 7 and 8 caught the attention of Hitler and Goebbels. On November 9, at the Munich reception for longtime Nazis,

1. Schutzstaffel-
Appell
der Gruppe Ost in Berlin
11., 12., 13. August

As head of party propaganda, Joseph Goebbels became proficient at swaying the masses toward Nazism. This Nazi election poster calls for Germans to join the Nazi Party.

the two men spoke about the "demonstrations." Goebbels's diary recorded the conversation:

> I go to the party reception in the Old Town Hall. Huge amount going on. I explain the matter to the Führer. He decides: let the demonstrations continue. Pull back the police. The Jews for once should get to feel the anger of the people. That's right. I immediately give corresponding directives to police and party.[8]

When Hitler left, Goebbels stood to address the audience. Banging his fist, he announced the death of vom Rath:

> I have news for you here tonight . . . to demonstrate what happens to a good German when he drops his guard for one moment. Ernst vom Rath was a good German . . . working for the good of our people in our embassy in Paris. Shall I tell you what happened to him? He was shot down! In the course of his duty, he went, unarmed and unsuspecting, to speak to a visitor at the embassy, and had two bullets pumped into him. He is now dead. . . . Do I need to tell you the race of the dirty swine

> who perpetrated this foul deed? A Jew! Tonight he lies in jail in Paris, claiming that he acted on his own; that he had no [other helpers]. But we know better, don't we? [9]

By the time Goebbels finished his speech, the national part of Kristallnacht had been launched. Goebbels's diary described what he thought and saw on his way back to his hotel:

> I wish to return to my hotel, and see a glow as red as blood. The synagogue is burning. . . . We only put out the fires when they endanger adjacent buildings. If not, they should be burned to the ground. . . . Reports come from all over the Reich. 50 synagogues, then 70 are on fire. The Fuehrer ordered 20-30 thousand Jews to be arrested. . . . Public anger is running wild. . . . They have to be given the possibility to vent their rage. . . . Driving to the hotel, windows are being smashed. Bravo, bravo. The synagogues burn like big old huts. There is no danger to German property. [10]

Joseph Goebbels gave a speech to many longtime Nazis after the assassination of Ernst vom Rath, blaming all Jews for the murder. Goebbels was known as a powerful speaker and appears here giving a speech in 1933.

The pogrom that Goebbels directed included the burning and looting of Jewish businesses, synagogues, and schools. The houses and apartments of Jewish families were ransacked, and their worldly goods destroyed and sometimes stolen. Tens of thousands of Jewish men and teenagers were arrested and sent to concentration camps. As synagogues burned, firefighters were instructed to fight the flames only when "Aryan" property was threatened. As Jews were beaten and otherwise tormented, police officers were told not to interfere.

KRISTALLNACHT INSTRUCTIONS FOR GESTAPO AND STATE POLICE

A few minutes before midnight, orders concerning the pogrom were telegraphed to Gestapo offices around Germany. The orders included:

> Actions against Jews, especially against their synagogues, will take place throughout the Reich shortly. They are not to be interfered with. . . . Preparations are to be made for the arrest of about 20,000 to 30,000 Jews in the Reich. Above all well-to-do Jews are to be selected. Detailed instructions will follow in the course of this night. . . . Should Jews in possession of weapons be encountered in the course of the action, the sharpest measures are to be taken.[11]

Only a few minutes later, one of Munich's synagogues was burning.

An hour and a half later, early in the morning of November 10, Gestapo offices received further orders:

> . . . demonstrations against the Jews are to be expected throughout the Reich in the present night . . . measures should be taken [that] will not endanger German life or property (i.e. synagogue burning only if there is no fire-danger to the surroundings). . . . Businesses and dwellings of Jews should only be destroyed, not plundered. The police are instructed to supervise this regulation and to arrest looters. . . . Special care is to be taken that in business streets non-Jewish businesses are absolutely secured against damage. . . . Foreign nationals— even if they are Jews—should not be molested. . . . Directly after the termination of the events of this night . . . as many Jews—especially the well-off ones—are to be arrested as can be accommodated in the available prison space. Above all only healthy, male Jews, not too old, are to be arrested. . . . Special care is to be taken that the Jews arrested on this order are not maltreated.[12]

The Nazi government was now ready to systematically destroy everything Jewish.

On November 10, at five o'clock in the afternoon, Goebbels called on the "entire population" to stop "any further demonstrations or action against the Jews." He stated, however, that the destruction had been "natural and fully justified" given the "brutal Jewish assassination in Paris."[13]

Goebbels's End

As the end of the war approached, Goebbels, his wife Magda, and six children stayed in a secret underground bunker with Hitler and his staff in Berlin. When word reached them on April 30, 1945, that the Russians were within one mile of the bunker, Hitler committed suicide.

The next night, Magda mixed a sleeping potion with her children's dinner, then administered a spoonful of poison to each one after they had fallen asleep. Once all six children were dead, Goebbels and his wife killed themselves.

The war had ended, and Goebbels's reign of terror was over forever.

3   Hannele Zürndorfer

Hannele Zürndorfer and her family were only one of two Jewish families in Gerresheim, a small town outside Dusseldorf. They felt as much German as they were Jewish. Her family celebrated Christmas and Easter as well as Chanukah and Passover. Christmas was a joyous celebration in her house, with carol-singing and mysterious presents waiting to be opened. Chanukah was more solemn, an occasion that her father always made "poignant and significant."[1]

But the anti-Jewish hatred spread by the Nazis began to have a negative impact on Hannele's happy childhood.

"The papers all carried cartoons lampooning the Jews with enormous, grotesque noses, furtive or greedy faces and big, slobbering lips," Hannele recalled in her autobiography, *The Ninth of November*. "Very gradually people started withdrawing from contact with us."[2]

Her best friend, Ella, attempted to remain friends, but a new girl in their neighborhood, Gisela, had other ideas. An enthusiastic supporter of the Nazis, Gisela "felt it was her duty to see that I was treated as a Jew ought to be."[3] Influenced by Gisela and others, Ella pulled away from Hannele and stopped being friends.

This illustration from the Nazi picture book entitled *Trust No Fox in the Green Meadow and No Jew on His Oath* displays the anti-Jewish hatred in Germany during Hannele's childhood.

Rising Tensions at School

Hannele also noticed a change at school. She and her classmates used to stand up and say good morning to their teacher as she entered the classroom. Now, the students had to salute Adolf Hitler instead, shouting, "Heil Hitler!" Hannele did not want to participate. Her teacher understood the dilemma Hannele faced and, in defiance of Nazi policy, privately told her that she did not have to join in.

By 1937, new laws prohibited Hannele from attending a German elementary school. She was forced to travel over an hour to a Jewish school that had been set up in Dusseldorf. The school

> was staffed with good teachers—they had, like the children, been thrown out of the state schools. . . . The syllabus was designed as preparation for emigration. Languages were given priority. . . . All the time children were leaving to emigrate with their families.[4]

She made a good friend named Inge at her new school. One day, when the school had vacation, the two girls agreed to spend the afternoon ice-skating at a nearby outdoor rink. When they arrived, they saw large signs that read:

> DOGS AND JEWS NOT PERMITTED. We hesitated. We were by then used to seeing "No Jews here!" notices everywhere. We had been looking forward to skating, it was a sunny afternoon, a school holiday and such opportunities were rare. The temptation was overwhelming . . . neither of us looked particularly Jewish; we both had blue eyes and light brown hair. So . . . we decided to go in . . . and had a thoroughly enjoyable afternoon.[5]

When Hannele told her father what she had done, he told her that she needed to have a "sense of pride and dignity" and not go anywhere where she would not be wanted.[6]

Kristallnacht

Whatever troubled Hannele about school and the restrictions placed on her life outside her home in Gerresheim, she still felt safe in her home. There she could "shut out the grey, fearsome streets with jackbooted Brownshirts who stamped like robots, marching, shouting, saluting, red-faced, with wild and bloodshot eyes. . . . Danger was outside. At home we were safe—I thought."[7]

The night that the national Kristallnacht pogrom began, her home was no longer a safe haven.

Around four o'clock in the morning, Hannele heard the

repeated sound of breaking glass and smashing dishes coming from the kitchen below. Then the china cabinet crashed to the floor. Hannele did not know what to think. Were burglars in the house? Was her family in the middle of an earthquake?

A young man on a motorcycle stares up at a sign posted in Germany that reads, "Jews are not welcome here." Signs segregating Jews from "Aryans" were posted all over Germany.

Hannele and her sister, Lotte, ran to their parents' bedroom, where they crawled into bed with them.

> *Seconds later there burst into this room a horde of violent monsters, their faces contorted into raving masks of hatred, some red, some pale, all screaming and shouting, eyes rolling, teeth bared, wild hands flailing, jackboots kicking. They were wielding axes, sledgehammers, stones, and knives. They rushed about the room smashing, throwing, trampling. It seemed to me that there were hundreds of them bursting through the door, though I believe there were, in fact, only a dozen.*[8]

The men threw a chair into the wardrobe mirror, slashed a treasured painting, and splintered anything wooden with their axes. One Nazi slid the marble top off a dressing table and threw it at Hannele's father. Another aimed an axe at the legs of Hannele's mother, but she was able to pull them away in time.

When there was nothing left to destroy in the bedroom, a small brown-shirted man leaned over the bed and whispered to Hannele and her sister, "Children don't look, don't look children. Hide your eyes. I am sorry. I had to do it."[9] Then he led the others from the room to other parts of the house, where their frenzied destruction continued:

No one moved. The sounds continued awhile and then there was silence, though my mind still heard the noise. But there was silence, complete and sudden, with only broken furniture groaning and settling into place. We listened to the silence for a long time, not daring to breathe, expecting them to return any minute to kill us all. But they did not return.[10]

The Zürndorfers' apartment was completely destroyed during Kristallnacht. This is the interior of a synagogue in Hechingen, Germany, that was torn apart during the pogrom.

Picking up the Pieces

The Zürndorfers' house was a shambles. When Hannele wrote about the experience later in life, she remembered certain images as if they were photographs:

> The piano on its side, its guts ripped out and scattered on the floor like the bones and sinews of some huge animal; every single oil painting hanging in strips out of its frame or lying impaled on the spikes of upturned furniture . . . books were torn, the pages scattered; furnishings were slashed with the stuffing welling out like flesh; old oak and walnut tables and chairs were legless; the carpets hacked, curtains torn down, floorboards splintered, and many windows smashed.[11]

Only the bedroom of Hannele and her sister had been spared; their beds were still whole. Scared and exhausted, the family lay down and tried to sleep until morning.

Hannele's favorite school teacher, Frau Rottger, came the following night with food, dinnerware, and clothing. But the most important thing she brought was "the feeling that we were not utterly alone in the world."[12]

Family members who lived in the United States and England pleaded with Mr. Zürndorfer to emigrate as soon as possible; they feared for the safety of the family if they remained in Germany any longer. But Mr. Zürndorfer did not seem interested at first:

> *I think quite honestly my father was stunned. For the moment he floundered. It meant recognizing the utter hopelessness of life in Germany. Everything he has spent his life in building . . . had been destroyed. How could he face such an absolute denial of his ideals?*[13]

Finally, he decided to make plans for the family's emigration.

Departing Germany

Hannele and Lotte received permission to emigrate to England, where they would live with relatives. Their parents would remain behind in Germany until their papers were approved. Then they would stop in England, collect their children, and head for the United States, where they planned to reside permanently.

Hannele and Lotte were placed on a *Kindertransport* train to the Netherlands, where they would take a boat across the English Channel. Their father was so concerned about their safety that he jumped aboard the train as it left the Dusseldorf station. He rode it all the way to the Dutch border, satisfied that his two daughters were on their way to safety.

In London, Hannele and her sister lived in a cramped attic apartment. When the German air force began to bomb

Two Jewish refugee children sit together after arriving in England on a Kindertransport from Germany on December 12, 1938. Hannele and Lotte were put on a Kindertransport by their parents and reached safety in England.

English cities, they were evacuated from London with many other children and sent to live with volunteer families in the countryside.

There, Hannele and Lotte longed for word that their parents would be coming to take them to the United States. In the end, the Zürndorfers were not able to get the proper papers to emigrate, and in October 1941, they were transported to the Lodz ghetto in Poland.

The Ending

In 1943, Hannele learned that her father had died of a heart attack in Lodz, but she was never able to find her mother. After the war, relatives filled in some missing details of her parents' life in Germany before they were transported to Lodz. They had been forced by Nazi decree to sell their house in Gerresheim to an Aryan family for much less than it was worth. Then they had to pay rent to live in the attic. When there were air raids, the new owners would not let the Zürndorfers take shelter in the basement.

Hannele eventually wrote two books about her childhood and now lives in Scotland. The elementary school in Gerresheim that she was forced to leave in 1937 still exists. In 2003, the school was renamed in her honor: the Hanna-Zürndorfer School.

4 Fred Spiegel

As a small child, Fred Spiegel enjoyed going to the park with his grandfather near his home in Dinslaken, Germany. One day, when he was four or five, his playtime in the park suddenly changed. In a book he wrote about his childhood experiences, he recalled that older children in the park

> . . . started to pick on me, tried to beat me up, threw stones and dirt on me, and called me "Dirty Jew." Then my grandfather's friends also started to curse him and he decided it was time to get out of the park. When I went home I asked my mother, "How come those kids call me 'Dirty Jew'? Am I dirty? I took a bath this morning." After a few more incidents, we did not go to the park anymore, even though it was almost our backyard.[1]

Instead, Fred's grandfather began to take him to a nearby Jewish orphanage to play with the children. Soon, he made new friends who did not torment and bully him because of his religion.

48

Kristallnacht

On November 10, 1938, Fred was six years old. That morning, as he looked out his window, he saw clouds of black smoke rising in the distance, a sight that was "scary and threatening."[2] No one, not even his mother, knew what was burning. He went upstairs, where a married couple named the Brockhausens rented an apartment from his family. Although the Brockhausens, as non-Jews, were forbidden by law to rent an apartment from a Jewish family, they had chosen to stay.

The Brockhausens told Fred that the synagogue was on fire. But they told him not to worry; fire engines were on the scene to put out the fire.

Suddenly, someone battered the main door to the Spiegel house; Fred heard glass shattering. He recalled:

Smoke clouds rise from the Boerneplatz synagogue in Frankfurt am Main, Germany, on November 10, 1938. Fred Spiegel watched the smoke rising from the synagogue in Dinslaken during Kristallnacht.

> *My sister and mother started to scream. I wanted to run downstairs but Mr. Brockhausen held me back. I could clearly hear things being smashed downstairs and being thrown out of the window onto the street below. Finally I went downstairs. . . . Upon entering, I found that many things had been totally destroyed, the windows broken, and much of our furniture and crystal was on the pavement below. My mother, sister, and Aunt Klara were standing on the balcony crying. My grandfather had been arrested and taken away by two policemen.*[3]

The police told the Spiegel family to accompany them. As they walked down the street, people standing on the sidewalks threw rocks and spit at them. They also saw their burning synagogue before they were taken to a Jewish school, where they were told to spend the night.

Moving to the Netherlands

A few days after Kristallnacht, their mother sent Fred and his sister Edith to live with relatives in the Netherlands. She hoped that she would be able to obtain visas for the family so that they could emigrate to the United States or Palestine (now Israel).

KRISTALLNACHT AT THE DINSLAKEN ORPHANAGE

A group portrait of Jewish girls at the orphanage in Dinslaken, Germany, prior to Kristallnacht.

The Jewish orphanage in Dinslaken was home to many of Fred's childhood playmates. Many years later, he discovered that on Kristallnacht the orphans were forced to march through the streets of Dinslaken. This *Judenparade* (a parade of Jews) was meant to humiliate and bully the children. The director of the orphanage kept a diary in which he recorded what happened:

> *The people of Dinslaken stood three and four deep along the sidewalk to await the Judenparade. Most people cursed and taunted us but on the faces of a few there was disgust at the proceedings. In front of the parade were two policemen, flanked by uniformed Nazis. The little children of the orphanage were forced to climb into a hay wagon and four older boys were forced to pull this wagon.[4]*

One orphan later reported that the children

> *were driven through the streets to a small schoolyard close to the [burned] synagogue. . . . There they joined other members of the local Jewish congregation. All were taken into a small schoolroom and forbidden to leave it. They had to spend the whole day there without food or water. That evening they were then taken to another building . . . [where] they spent eight further days. . . .[5]*

Fred also learned that most of the children from the Dinslaken Orphanage did not survive the war.

51

Eventually, she received a visa to travel to England to work as a maid, but she was not allowed to take her children. Fred and his sister stayed in the Netherlands, hoping to be reunited soon.

Eight months later, Germany invaded the Netherlands, on May 10, 1940. The Gestapo wanted to arrest Fred's uncle. When they could not find him, they beat Fred's aunt to make her confess his whereabouts. To save themselves, his uncle and aunt went into hiding.

Fred and Edith were sent to stay with other relatives—Uncle Max and Cousin Alfred—who lived in a small farm village named Dinxperlo. Although many other Jews around the Netherlands were arrested and sent to concentration camps, the Jews of the tiny hamlet of Dinxperlo seemed to live in a protective bubble.

Then in 1942, on the eve of Yom Kippur (the holiest day of the Jewish calendar), the Jews of Dinxperlo were worshipping in their synagogue when a man burst into the services with news that the Gestapo was coming to arrest Jewish men.

The cantor (the man who led the prayers) continued praying, but the men in the congregation began to leave. Soon, only Fred and the other boys remained. Fred never saw anyone from the synagogue again after that night because most were taken to Vught, a concentration camp in the southern Netherlands.

Fred, Edith, and Uncle Max and his family were arrested on April 10, 1943, and taken to Vught as well. Six weeks later, they were sent to another Dutch camp, Westerbork.

Missing the Transport

The next morning, when they arrived in Westerbork, Fred and his cousin Alfred were told that they were to be placed on the train for a "resettlement or work camp" in eastern Europe. In truth, the train was headed either for Sobibor or Auschwitz, where death by gassing awaited most of the passengers. But the victims did not know this. At first, Fred and Alfred did as they were told and

> . . . we walked towards the train, carrying the few belongings that we were allowed to take with us. It was dawn and the walk to the train was very scary. Nearly everybody was crying, especially the little children. The people not going on that train were under total curfew and could neither leave their barracks nor look out of the few windows.[6]

At the train, Dutch police who worked in the camp began to push everyone on board. Although most people entered the train cars quietly, Fred suddenly began to scream, "I don't want to go onto this train."[7] His cousin also began to yell the same words.

A nearby SS guard asked a Dutch policeman why the boys were yelling. When he was told that the boys were frightened, he ordered that the boys get off the train. They were taken to a small holding cell, and the train left without them. Only later, when he was much older, did Fred realize that he and his cousin had avoided being sent to Sobibor. As an adult, he researched what happened to the Jews sent from Westerbork to Sobibor and found that "[b]etween March and August 1943, about 35,000 Jews were transported from Westerbork to Sobibor. Only nineteen people are known to have survived."[8]

Later, his cousin Alfred and his family were transported to Sobibor; they, too, died in the camp's gas chamber. But Uncle Max had gone to great lengths to save Fred and his sister. Before he was shipped to Sobibor, Uncle Max spoke to the camp commandant and showed him letters that Fred's mother had written. He told the camp commandant that Fred and his sister were British citizens. This meant that they should be considered "foreign nationals" and exempt from transport.

At Bergen-Belsen

On January 11, 1944, Fred and his sister were sent to Bergen-Belsen, where they were housed in the exchange camp. Because the Nazis believed that they were foreign nationals, Fred and his sister were possible "exchanges." The Germans planned to use them to trade for German prisoners of war. At Bergen-Belsen, they experienced much worse conditions than at Westerbork:

> . . . we got little food—starvation rations. The sanitary conditions were terrible, almost non-existent—a small washroom by each barrack with little water. There were no showers. . . . In order to take a shower, the guards had to take us to a different

As the end of the war neared, Fred and his sister were forced onto another transport with many other prisoners. After a six-day journey, German guards opened the train doors and told the prisoners that American troops might be nearby. Then the guards gave them some moldy bread and left. Soon, American soldiers approached the train. "We must have looked like nightmare figures, monsters from something out of science fiction, apparitions arisen from the grave," Fred wrote. "They obviously had never seen inmates from concentration camps."[10]

Finding a Lost Childhood

A few months after the war ended, Fred and Edith were reunited with their mother in England. In 1952, Fred emigrated to Israel and served in its army. Eventually, he moved to America

Although Fred vowed never to set foot in Germany again, he took his wife and children to Europe in 1989 to visit places from his childhood: the relative's houses in the Netherlands, the camps at Vught and Westerbork, his hometown of Dinslaken, and the camp at Bergen-Belsen.

The most moving part of the trip came in Dinslaken. There, the mayor escorted Fred and his family through the town and showed them the Jewish cemetery where his father and grandmother were buried. Fred became friends with the mayor and began to visit Dinslaken once a year. In 1993, the mayor organized a reunion of the Dinslaken Jewish community on the fifty-fifth anniversary of Kristallnacht. The reunion coincided with the unveiling of a memorial to the Jewish community.

At home in the United States, Fred spoke to students about his childhood experiences. During these visits, he was asked:

> *"Did you ever return to Germany and what is your attitude towards the Germans?" I always tell them, I cannot blame today's generation for what their grandparents may have done. I also believe you have to forgive, but never forget.*[11]

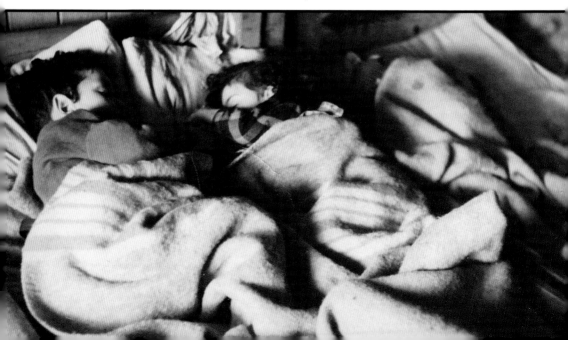

Young children sleep in barracks at the Bergen-Belsen camp after the British liberated it on April 15, 1945. Fred Spiegel suffered from horrible conditions at the camp until his liberation.

5 Ernest Fontheim

Ernest Fontheim and his family were well integrated into German life in their Berlin neighborhood. Although they observed high holy days of Judaism, Ernest Fontheim's more vivid childhood memories were of Christmas. His family celebrated the holiday every year, with a Christmas tree and presents from Santa Claus. In fact, Fontheim grew up knowing very little about Judaism, except that he was considered Jewish.

A Witness to a Beating

Then came Kristallnacht. When they woke up on Thursday, November 10, Ernest and his family had no idea that terrible destruction had occurred in Germany during the night. The family's apartment was untouched.

On his way to school that morning, he did not see anything unusual. At school, he realized that something was wrong, since many students were not in attendance. Then the teachers told the students to go home—individually, not in groups—so as not to attract attention from gangs of Nazis still roaming the streets.

Ernest hopped on the train home, but this train passed his synagogue. What he saw out the train window, he told an interviewer for the United States Holocaust Memorial Museum in 1997, "was one of the worst horror shocks of my life. It was a

This synagogue in Bielefeld, Germany, is destroyed by fire during Kristallnacht. Ernest Fontheim watched his synagogue burn down in Berlin.

beautiful building with . . . three huge domes . . . and from the center dome came a huge thick column of smoke."[1]

Without thinking about the consequences, he got off the train at the next stop and ran back to the synagogue. A mob of onlookers stood across the street watching the building burn. Fontheim recalled what he saw:

A pile of Hebrew prayer books and other Jewish texts damaged by fire at the synagogue in Bobenhausen, Germany. The Nazis desecrated many Jewish religious texts during Kristallnacht.

> [T]he fire department . . . hosing down adjacent buildings so to prevent the flames from doing damage to Germany property and no hose was directed at the synagogue. . . . And then, there were many anti-Semitic shouts from the mob . . . like . . . "throw out the Jews" or "kill the Jews" and it never occurred to me that I was one in the middle of the mob.[2]

Someone in the crowd shouted that a Jew was living in a nearby house that faced the synagogue. Members of the crowd stormed the apartment building and began breaking down the man's door.

> I couldn't see what was happening there. And all I could think was I hope that the door is going to hold . . . but of course it didn't and I could hear splintering wood and then . . . silence. . . . And then I heard shouts like, "get them, get them," and then there was an elderly man . . . he had a huge bald head . . . and then from all sides there were blows and his face soon was completely bloodied.[3]

Ernest made his way back to the train safely, but the incident had been a major turning point in his life.

THE MURDER OF SUSANNA STERN

The first murder of a Jew on Kristallnacht was reported to Joseph Goebbels around two o'clock in the morning of November 10. Although the killing of Jews had not been officially encouraged, Goebbels was not surprised and told the person who reported the murder "not to get so worked up about the death of a Jew. In the next days, thousands more would kick the bucket."[4] Other murders did follow, but Nazi authorities decided not to prosecute any murderer as long as the person had not acted "for selfish reasons."[5]

Eventually, twenty-six SA members were charged with killing Jews on Kristallnacht.[6] Among them was SA officer Adolf Frey, who murdered an eighty-one-year-old widow named Susanna Stern in Elberstadt, Germany.

According to his court testimony, Frey arrived at Mrs. Stern's house around eight in the morning and ordered her to accompany him. When she repeatedly refused, Frey shot her. He told the court that after he had fired the gun once

> Stern collapsed on the sofa. She leaned back and grabbed her chest with her hands. Right away I shot the second time, this time aiming at the head. As a result, Mrs. Stern slid off the sofa and turned over. She then lay immediately in front of the sofa with her head turned to the left, toward the windows. . . . My comrade . . . turned the head of Mrs. Stern . . . in order to see where she had been hit. . . . In order to make sure that Mrs. Stern was dead, I fired from a distance of approximately ten centimeters at the middle of her forehead. . . .[7]

Frey was never convicted because proceedings were suspended on October 10, 1940, but his recorded testimony revealed the truth of what had happened.

Avoiding the Gestapo

Ernest stayed home from school the next day. Although he did not seem in danger, his father was. An Aryan colleague in his law office warned Ernest's father "not to go back to his office or . . . to his own apartment and . . . stay at places where there are no Jewish males."[8] Mr. Fontheim went in hiding at the house of his widowed sister.

Ernest told the interviewer that

> . . . the Gestapo came both to our apartment and also to the office to inquire and, of course, we told them he left and didn't tell us where he was going, and in those days the Gestapo still took these relatively stupid excuses and just reappeared a few random times maybe hoping to catch him. . . .[9]

Eventually, his father was able to return home, and, by hiding, he had temporarily avoided arrest. As the Nazi crackdown continued, Mr. Fontheim was disbarred from the law and could no longer earn an income. Ernest's parents tried to emigrate now, but they had delayed too long. When World War II began in September 1939, the country's borders were closed, and the Fontheims were trapped in Germany.

A group of male Jews are forced to do demeaning exercises in Germany on November 11, 1938. Jews were routinely persecuted on the street during the violent pogrom.

Forced Labor for the War

In early 1941, Ernest was ordered to work at a Siemens electronics factory making war materials. Many other Jews were forced to work there. Segregated in one room where they were watched constantly, they were not allowed to use the lunchroom and could only use the toilet twice a day, at 9:00 and at 1:00.

Ernest was resourceful through this period of his life. Although new laws required Jews to wear the yellow Star of David on their outer clothing, Ernest and his friends developed a way to avoid doing so. At the time, double-breasted jackets could be buttoned either on the left or the right side. They would go out wearing the yellow star openly, then enter an apartment building and rebutton their jackets, without the yellow star on display. They could then look like German Aryans.

Although Ernest hated his forced labor at the factory, his work there prevented him from being transported to a concentration camp. His parents, however, had no such protection.

They were arrested twice and scheduled for a transport. The first time, in April 1942, his father, expecting that this might occur, was prepared to commit suicide. He was not in good health and wanted to prevent himself from suffering more. Using medicine that his doctor had given him, his father attempted suicide.

The medicine put him in a coma, and he was taken to a Jewish hospital. His family was sent back home, and his father was eventually released from the hospital. His attempted suicide saved his life, for awhile. But, on December 24, 1942, his family was arrested for a second and final time.

Again, his father took the medicine to kill himself, but this time the Gestapo completed the arrest.

Fearing for his own safety, Ernest went into hiding in early 1943 with a few other Jews in a rural bungalow. The house was owned by a woman who had worked for Ernest's father some thirty-five miles southeast of Berlin. Through help from the underground, Ernest was able to get identity papers that showed that he was a German (not a Jew) working at a defense plant in Berlin. For more than two years, Ernest survived with his new identity. Then he got word that a neighbor suspected that he and

Ernest Fontheim worked at a Siemens electronics factory making war materials for the Germans. In this photo, forced laborers work at another Siemens factory in Bobrek, a sub-camp of Auschwitz.

the other people he lived with were foreign spies and planned to tell the Gestapo. In March 1945, just six weeks before the end of the war, Ernest and the others left the house and headed for Berlin, where they survived the rest of the war.

After the War

After the war, he learned that his parents and sister had been transported to Auschwitz, a death camp run by the Nazis, and murdered there. He was haunted by his imagination of the events.

Two years after the war ended, Ernest was given permission to emigrate to the United States. He started college in New York, then transferred to a college in Missouri. Eventually, he earned a PhD and worked as a scientist at the University of Michigan.

6　Marianne Strauss

As Marianne Strauss grew up in Essen, Germany, she was unaware of any prejudice. She attended a Jewish school, but felt as much German as Jewish.

In April 1933, however, she transferred to a non-Jewish girls' grammar school. There, she learned about antisemitism. She "heard for the first time the word 'Jew' being hissed behind my back."[1] Most of her classmates were members of the *Bund Deutscher Mädel* (BDM), the girls' branch of the Hitler Youth.

Kristallnacht

On Kristallnacht, Marianne's neighborhood was quiet. In fact, she did not know that Essen's synagogue had been burned or that shop windows had been smashed until she went to school the next day. A classmate greeted her by yelling, "You old Jew, get lost, you've no business here."[2] Then she hit Marianne on the head with a heavy book. A short time later, Marianne went home and never returned to the school.

When they learned that 319 Jewish men had been arrested in Essen, Marianne's father and uncle decided to go into hiding.[3] Members of the Gestapo visited the Strauss home looking for the two men. They told Marianne "that if they didn't turn up they would take my mother and me. That brought my father and my uncle out pretty quickly."[4] On November 12, 1938, Marianne's father and uncle turned themselves into the police and were taken to Dachau.

Some three weeks later, they were released. Almost immediately, the family received a bill for the tax on the damages done to Jewish buildings during Kristallnacht. The first of three installment payments was due December 15. Although they paid on time, the Nazi government even billed them an extra late fee.

The family wanted to leave Germany, but their visa applications for Australia and New Zealand were rejected. Then, twelve days after they were approved for emigration to England, Britain and Germany went to war, and all emigration was stopped. The Strauss family could not leave Germany.

Young members of the *Bund Deutscher Mädel* (BDM) wave Nazi flags during a rally In Vienna, Austria, in 1938. When Marianne Strauss transferred to a non-Jewish girls' school, she was harassed by members of the BDM.

Almost Deported

In October 1941, Marianne's parents were two of 250 Jews in Essen scheduled to be deported to the ghetto in Lodz, Poland.[5] They spent a day packing. They were allowed to take " . . . up to [100 marks] one suitcase containing household goods, a complete set of clothing, bedclothes, and food for eight days. Valuables, other money, jewelry (apart from wedding rings), pets, and ration cards could not be taken."[6]

On the designated morning, October 26, 1941, a Nazi official came to the house, told the family to wait outside with their

A group of Jews from Prague, Czechoslovakia, move their belongings through the streets of the Lodz ghetto in Poland. The Strauss family was supposed to be sent to Lodz, but managed to avoid the deportation order.

belongings, and then sealed the house. They were told to carry their luggage down the street where a tram would take them to the train station. Marianne recalled:

> I shall never forget the moment when we were standing there and the people were all being loaded into the tram. In front of everyone, two Gestapo officials, notorious officials from the Gestapo headquarters . . . told my family that we were not to get on but should go back home.[7]

Why had the Strauss family been spared from the transport? Quite simply, Marianne's father had agreed to go to the United States and become a spy for the Nazi intelligence agency named *Abwehr*. Perhaps it was a ploy that Mr. Strauss used to make sure that his family might be able to emigrate to the United States. Still, the Gestapo stopped the family's deportation, and they were allowed to return home.

The Transport

By 1943, the Strauss family were the last Jews remaining in Essen. The rest had emigrated or been deported to concentration camps. They still hoped to be allowed to leave Germany, possibly to escape to Sweden. But on August 31, 1943, two Gestapo officials arrived and told the family that they had two hours to get ready to leave. They would be transported "to the East." Marianne recalled the day it happened:

> *[The Gestapo] did not let us out of their sight. The allotted two hours were filled with feverish packing of the few things we were allowed to take. . . . Then came my moment. The two officials disappeared into the basement, probably to find some loot. . . . Unable to say goodbye to my parents, my brother, and my relatives, I followed the impulse of the moment and ran out of the house just as I was, with a few hundred mark notes which my father had stuffed into my pockets moments before. I ran for my life, expecting a pistol shot behind me any minute.[8]*

Marianne was amazed, but nothing happened. In a short time, she found herself under the protection of the Bund, an anti-Nazi underground organization (federation). The Gestapo took the Strauss family to an Essen prison, awaiting Marianne's capture. Marianne learned of their imprisonment and faced a nightmare:

> *I thought: there is nothing I can do. If I join them that only does the Gestapo a favor, not my parents or me, because the Gestapo can then send them off to wherever they send them off to. Whereas [if I don't join my family], my family is still here,*

She tried calling influential people in town who had helped the family before, but she was warned not to call again. There was nothing she could do. When Marianne did not appear in a few days, her family was transported to Theresienstadt, a concentration camp in Czechoslovakia. She later learned that her parents were transported from Theresienstadt to Auschwitz and murdered in the gas chambers in July 1944.

Marianne's family was transported to Theresienstadt, and then they were sent to Auschwitz, where they were murdered in 1944. This painting of the Vltava River in Prague, Czechoslovakia, by Bedrich Fritta was created in Theresienstadt, where he made many paintings depicting life in the camp. He was also deported to Auschwitz and died in the gas chambers in October 1944.

Eluding the Nazis

For the next eighteen months, Marianne traveled with members of the Bund around the country. People who allowed Marianne into their homes had to explain to neighbors and relatives who she was and why she had come to stay with them. Then they had to answer many questions: Where was her family? Why wasn't she working? For this reason, she and her Bund companions never remained more than three weeks with any family.

Without proper identification, she was unable to obtain ration cards for food. But she had "some money and access to suitcases containing clothes and linen that my parents had hidden some weeks before their deportation, so I was able to barter their clothing with farmers in the country in exchange for food or clothing."[10] Occasionally, she made trips back to Essen to visit the Jürgens family. Acquaintances of her parents, they had agreed to allow the Strauss family to store many of their household goods and personal possessions until the war was over. Marianne would visit the Jürgens to open the storage trunks and remove items that she could trade. Unfortunately, the Jürgens also removed items from her parents' trunks.

When she was in Essen, she hid in a house from where she could see a Catholic church on Sunday. Marianne recalled that the Jürgens would attend Sunday services

. . . and it was really quite ironic that they were praying there . . . and I could see them coming in and praying. Little did

> *they know that I was just around the*
> *corner from them. They went to church*
> *and they prayed, then they went home and*
> *robbed a little more.*[11]

After the War

When World War II ended, Marianne wanted to leave Germany and applied for permission to emigrate to England. Eventually, she received permission. There, she married and had two children.

Near the end of her life, Professor Mark Roseman interviewed Strauss for a book that he was writing about her. When she was asked about the Holocaust, she told Roseman that she believed it could happen anywhere:

> *[Y]ou look at television every night and*
> *you see the atrocities that are going on*
> *now everywhere, in every part of the world.*
> *Well, after a while, you become immune.*
> *It's the most dreadful thing . . . how people*
> *come to think that [the death of] six*
> *million makes an enormous difference*
> *from sixty or six thousand. It's what you*
> *do, not how many you do it to—that is at*
> *the root of the thing. The enormity for me*
> *lies in the fact that it happened at all—*
> *and that it is still happening.*[12]

7 Jurgen Herbst

An only child in a German Christian family, Jurgen Herbst enjoyed playing with his toy soldiers at his home in Wolfenbüttel. Sometimes he and his father would play with the soldiers, fighting imaginary battles. Other times, his father would tell him about his own experiences as a soldier in World War I. Because of his father's stories, Jurgen pictured soldiers as brave and loyal.

As he grew up, however, he encountered a very different kind of soldier in his town: brown-shirted soldiers who belonged to Hitler's SA troops. Jurgen realized that they were not well-liked by everyone:

> Whenever I had seen . . . real soldiers in field gray uniforms, and whenever I heard people talk about soldiers . . . people applauded and said good things about them. But . . . where the soldiers wore brown uniforms, some people hissed and booed. How could they do that, I wondered, if the men they booed were soldiers?[1]

His father, however, did not join the SA or the Nazi Party, something that puzzled Jurgen. He realized that his father did not respect Hitler. At one point, his father even warned him never to join the SS. However, when he was ten years old, Jurgen was obliged to become a member of the *Jungvolk*, a Hitler Youth organization intended for ten- to thirteen-year-old boys. He did not enjoy the meetings, and his mother would occasionally write notes excusing him. Missing the meetings made him happy.

A Burning Synagogue

On the morning of November 10, 1938, Jurgen was on his way to school when he heard the clanging bells of fire engines. They seemed to come from the part of town where his father worked in a library. Before he could begin to worry,

In this photo, six-year-old Jurgen Herbst carries a cone-shaped bag full of candy, as was custom for the first day of school in Germany. As a young boy, Jurgen and his father liked to fight imaginary battles.

he noticed that the front window of a leather clothing and shoe store was broken.

> *It was the only store window in which I had noticed before a red and white sign stuck in the corner which said: "Germans: Buy German—Don't Patronize a Jewish Business." Now, the jagged slivers of glass aroused my curiosity. . . . I walked across the street and then stared at the ladies' purses, shoes, and gloves that lay . . . covered with pulverized glass. And there, resting among the still well-polished pumps and slippers, lay half a brick. . . . I wondered why nobody had come to pick up the brick, sweep up the glass, and install some plywood . . . to protect the merchandise. . . . I figured an accident had happened in the night.*[2]

He hurried to school, anxious to tell his friends what he had seen. There, he and his friends decided to go see the burning building, joining a stream of others who wanted to see the blaze. When Jurgen turned the last corner, he was stunned:

> *And there we saw the synagogue or, more correctly, what was left of it. The red walls, the black slate roof, the well-kept lawn—the*

building . . . was gone. A burnt-out shell of smoke-blackened bricks, empty holes where the windows had been, a collapsed roof from whose splintered rafters plumes of black smoke drifted upward—that was all that remained. . . . Across the street . . . a fire engine was parked. The hoses were rolled up; the firefighters sat on or leaned against their truck, dozing and staring wordlessly at the scarred ruin.[3]

Damaged Jewish storefronts in Berlin after Kristallnacht. Jurgen Herbst did not understand why no one had cleaned up the Jewish store he passed on his way to school.

Nearby, an SS soldier stood smoking a cigarette. A man in the crowd called out to the soldier, "Solide deutsche Maßarbeit" (that is, "solid German craftsmanship").[4]

Jurgen did not understand this comment at all. "A fire," he thought, " . . . was not a piece of craftsmanship. It was an accident, a mishap, a disaster to boot, but not a piece of workmanship. I wondered what the man had meant."[5]

Another man in the crowd called out, "The firefighters were too late, I suppose?"

Another answered, "Firefighters? For such a fire, you don't call firefighters . . . firefighters can't do much with such a fire."[6]

Jurgen did not understand why the fire was not extinguished.

Understanding Kristallnacht

At school, later that morning, his teachers did not discuss what had happened, but, during recess, the students recounted the details of what they had seen and heard. Jurgen listened to a group of older boys talk about the disturbing arrest of a Jewish family: a four-year-old boy named Albert Morgenstern and his parents. Their furniture and belongings had been thrown out the windows onto the street. Then they had been taken away in a police van.

Jurgen wanted to know more, but recess was over.

By the time he went home for lunch, he was bursting with questions. When his mother asked what was new in school that day, Jurgen began to tell her what he had seen and heard. When he was done, his mother turned to him and said:

A GERMAN FIREFIGHTER REMEMBERS

Firefighters spray their hoses on a nearby house as local residents watch a synagogue burn down in Ober-Ramstadt, Germany. The firefighters tried to save the surrounding "Aryan" property while allowing the synagogue to burn to the ground.

A German firefighter from Laupheim, Germany, remembered Kristallnacht in a letter that he wrote.

Around five o'clock in the morning of November 10, the firefighter, whose name has never been given, was sleeping when the fire alarm rang. He rode his bicycle to the fire station where he learned that the synagogue was on fire. At first, he and the other firefighters were not permitted to take the fire engines out.

Eventually we were allowed to take the fire engines out, but only very slowly. We were ordered not to use any water till the whole synagogue was burned down. Many of us did not like to do that, but we had to be careful not to voice our opinions, because "the enemy is listening."[7]

As the firefighters waited, the SS rounded up Jews who lived nearby and

dragged them in front of the Synagogue, where they had to kneel down and put their hands above their heads. I saw with my own eyes how one old Jew was dragged down and pushed to his knees. Then the arsonists came in their brown uniforms to admire the results of their destruction.[8]

As he watched, the firefighter had one overwhelming thought: "When would it be our turn? Will the same thing happen to our Protestant and Catholic Churches!"[9]

> *"Do you know, Jurgen, if you had been Albert Morgenstern, you would have been torn from your bed last night; you, your father, and I would have been pushed down the staircase, and all your toys and books would have been thrown on the street. Had you been born a little Jewish boy, this would have happened to you last night."*[10]

Jurgen was shocked by his mother's revelation. He kept picturing himself and his parents being shoved down the stairs. Over and over again, when he was doing his homework, when he was trying to sleep at night, when he was at *Jungvolk* meetings, or attending school, he saw the image of the family falling down the steps. Sometimes he would hear a teacher mention the "Jewish danger" and other phrases that made Jews seem "so hateful to . . . Germans."[11] But he did not understand why.

Questions and Answers

He began to ask more questions about what he had seen. "Had Albert Morgenstern and his parents chosen to be Jews? Did they deserve to be punished just for being who they were? Why was I supposed to applaud that punishment?"[12]

He realized that for some unknown reason there was a difference between being German and being a Jew.

Jurgen Herbst was a member of the Hitler Youth. This is a page from a Hitler Youth identity book.

One day, he asked his mother if she knew any Jews besides the Morgensterns. Her answer shocked him: His piano teacher, a person he liked very much, was Jewish. But she was married to an "Aryan" man, a "pure-blooded" German according to the Nazi view. That made her safe from arrest for a time.

Still, Jurgen was confused: Should he continue piano lessons with a Jewish teacher? His mother reminded him that his friend Dieter, who was the leader of a hundred boys in *Jungvolk*, also took piano lessons from the same teacher. Finally, because he "could not think of anything that would turn her into an enemy," Jurgen continued his piano lessons.[13]

Defining the Enemy

Armed with the knowledge that he knew Jews and that they were people he respected, Jurgen struggled with the definition of "enemies."

At school his textbooks told him

that Jews were our enemies and that we must always be on guard against them. . . . There were signs in some shop windows that said: "Juden Unerwünscht" (Jews not desired), although . . . the proprietor of the paper store . . . where I bought my school supplies . . . had refused to put up such a sign. . . . At our Jungvolk meetings and when we marched through town we even sang a song about sending all the Jews

> to Jerusalem and, by chopping off their legs, making sure that they could not come back.[14]

What puzzled Jurgen most was that these so-called enemies lived next door, not in other countries like England or France, which were considered the political foes of Germany. Jurgen thought "it was only natural that we were being trained to battle Englishmen and Frenchmen in the field as soldiers."[15] But he did not understand why he was supposed to hate Jews:

> I wasn't ready to hate anybody. From what I had learned . . . the German soldier never hated his enemies. He fought them bravely in valiant battles, but he knew that his adversaries were just as brave battlers as he. . . . Soldiers, no matter of what country, were supposed to respect each other. . . . This business of hating enemies struck me and my classmates and quite a few of my fellow Jungvolk friends as rather unsoldierly.[16]

Becoming a Traitor

When Jurgen was thirteen, he became a *Jungvolkführer*, or the leader of a group of ten- to thirteen-year-old boys in *Jungvolk*.

At sixteen, he became an instructor for the Hitler Youth Leadership Training School. But he continued to question the principles of the Hitler Youth movement.

One day, early in his stay at the school, the principal told the teen instructors that a member of the Nazi Party could "never be a Christian! Christianity is treason against the German state! The church is a plague boil on the body of our people!"[17]

The statement troubled Jurgen greatly. He wondered how he could be a Nazi and go to church. He could not do both or he would be leading a "double life." He chose his religion and silently renounced Nazism:

At sixteen, Jurgen Herbst became an instructor in the Hitler Youth Leadership Training School, but he questioned Nazi principles. In this photo, Hitler Youth members march in a parade, as the leader of the Hitler Youth, Baldur von Schirach (right), salutes them.

was so shocked by the destruction that it seemed to him
Nazis had committed a murder. Sensing that he was in
e kept his anger inside and silently repeated a prayer
Bible, "Rise up, Lord, and scatter your enemies. . . ."[2]
that God might stop the destruction of the synagogue,
completely ruined.

t

r, on November 11, two Gestapo agents came to his
ome at six in the morning. Apparently working from a
nes, the Gestapo asked for Arnold and his uncle Bruno,
ted them both without any explanation.

and his uncle were taken to the main police station in
There, they were placed in a cell with other Jewish men
—"practically the entire male Jewish population of . . .
ranging from the age of eighteen to sixty-five years."[3]
isoners did not have access to a bathroom, only one pail
her. Blum remembered:

> ere confined in this crowded, stinking
> for several hours, standing while
> pressed together ever closer, as more
> nore Jews were added. There were
> ered conversations, recounting the
> us day's events, and speculations as
> fate in store for us. The cell door was
> d only to admit more prisoners.[4]

> . . . I could no longer live that double life.
> I could no longer wear the brown shirt of
> the Jungvolk and go to church on
> Sundays. . . . I had to make a choice. . . .
> Choose the party, the brown uniform, the
> Hitler Youth, or . . . the church. . . . If I was
> to live with myself, my family, my friends
> . . . there really was no choice to make—the
> choice had been made long ago.[18]

A Sad Farewell

A few months before the end of the war, he was called for basic military training. He was happy to be a soldier—but he wanted to be a good soldier, not a Nazi. He was glad when the war ended.

He returned home for a bittersweet reunion with his mother. His father had died while serving in the army, and his mother's health was failing. Even so, she took steps to help Jurgen with his education. She made sure that he finished his high school education. With his diploma, he was able to enter a college that trained teachers.

In 1948, Jurgen faced a new dilemma. His mother was close to death, but he had been chosen to participate in a seven-week international student seminar in the United States. This opportunity might allow Jurgen to complete his education in the United States:

From her hospital bed, his mother made him promise that he would go to the United States no matter what; she did not want her impending death to stop him from having a better life. He spent three days with her at the hospital. It was the last time that he would see her.

He stayed in the United States, where he became a professor of education at the University of Wisconsin. Eventually, he wrote a book about his childhood experiences, entitled *Requiem for a German Past: A Boyhood Among the Nazis.*

8 Arnold Blur

Sixteen years old at the time Blum lived with his mother Stuttgart, Germany. On th 1938, he stood helplessly as the Stutt ground. The American consul for St of the synagogue in Stuttgart and oth

> *. . . I could no longer live that double life. I could no longer wear the brown shirt of the Jungvolk and go to church on Sundays. . . . I had to make a choice. . . . Choose the party, the brown uniform, the Hitler Youth, or . . . the church. . . . If I was to live with myself, my family, my friends . . . there really was no choice to make—the choice had been made long ago.*[18]

A Sad Farewell

A few months before the end of the war, he was called for basic military training. He was happy to be a soldier—but he wanted to be a good soldier, not a Nazi. He was glad when the war ended.

He returned home for a bittersweet reunion with his mother. His father had died while serving in the army, and his mother's health was failing. Even so, she took steps to help Jurgen with his education. She made sure that he finished his high school education. With his diploma, he was able to enter a college that trained teachers.

In 1948, Jurgen faced a new dilemma. His mother was close to death, but he had been chosen to participate in a seven-week international student seminar in the United States. This opportunity might allow Jurgen to complete his education in the United States:

> *This unexpected news threw me into inner turmoil. There was no question in my mind that such an invitation was the greatest gift I could have possibly received. I wanted to go. But could I? How could I leave my mother when she was so desperately ill and there existed the real possibility that I might never see her again?*[19]

From her hospital bed, his mother made him promise that he would go to the United States no matter what; she did not want her impending death to stop him from having a better life. He spent three days with her at the hospital. It was the last time that he would see her.

He stayed in the United States, where he became a professor of education at the University of Wisconsin. Eventually, he wrote a book about his childhood experiences, entitled *Requiem for a German Past: A Boyhood Among the Nazis*.

8 Arnold Blum

Sixteen years old at the time of Kristallnacht, Arnold Blum lived with his mother, grandmother, and uncle in Stuttgart, Germany. On the morning of November 10, 1938, he stood helplessly as the Stuttgart synagogue burned to the ground. The American consul for Stuttgart described the burning of the synagogue in Stuttgart and other nearby cities:

The doors of the synagogues were forced open. Certain sections of the building and furnishings were drenched with petrol and set on fire. Bibles, prayer books, and other sacred things were thrown into the flames. Then the local fire brigades were notified. In Stuttgart, the city officials ordered the fire brigade to save the archives and other written material having a bearing on vital statistics. Otherwise, the fire brigades confined their activities to preventing the flames from spreading [to nearby buildings]. In a few hours the synagogues were, in general, heaps of smoking ruins.[1]

Blum was so shocked by the destruction that it seemed to him that the Nazis had committed a murder. Sensing that he was in danger, he kept his anger inside and silently repeated a prayer from the Bible, "Rise up, Lord, and scatter your enemies. . . ."[2] He hoped that God might stop the destruction of the synagogue, but it was completely ruined.

Arrest

A day later, on November 11, two Gestapo agents came to his family's home at six in the morning. Apparently working from a list of names, the Gestapo asked for Arnold and his uncle Bruno, then arrested them both without any explanation.

Blum and his uncle were taken to the main police station in Stuttgart. There, they were placed in a cell with other Jewish men and boys—"practically the entire male Jewish population of . . . Stuttgart, ranging from the age of eighteen to sixty-five years."[3]

The prisoners did not have access to a bathroom, only one pail in the corner. Blum remembered:

> We were confined in this crowded, stinking place for several hours, standing while being pressed together ever closer, as more and more Jews were added. There were whispered conversations, recounting the previous day's events, and speculations as to the fate in store for us. The cell door was opened only to admit more prisoners.[4]

SS guards force a large group of Jews to march down the street in Baden-Baden, Germany, after their arrest during Kristallnacht. These men were deported to the Sachsenhausen concentration camp. Arnold Blum was arrested and taken to Dachau.

Taken to Dachau

Eventually, Blum and the other prisoners were taken on buses for a three-hour ride to Dachau, a concentration camp near Munich. They were told to stand in formation in an area outside the camp as the buses were unloaded. In all, approximately eleven thousand Jewish men and boys were taken to Dachau.[5]

Blum watched how a prisoner on a nearby bus was singled out for particularly brutal treatment:

One man, who had apparently lost consciousness on the trip, was removed from the bus by an SS man pulling him by the ankles. This caused the man's head to hit each of the steps leading down from the bus. . . . After being dumped on the ground he flailed his arms and legs through the air, thereby inadvertently kicking his tormentor. The latter, in a blind rage, jumped on his victim, stomping and kicking him into submission with his hobnailed boots.[6]

Marched inside the camp about mid-afternoon, the men and boys were then made to stand at attention until nine o'clock that night. Unable to use a toilet, many of the prisoners wet their pants. After the men were ordered to their barracks, they were told to remove their shoes before entering the building and arrange them neatly outside; they would be able to retrieve them the following morning. That night, so many men were crammed into the barracks that many of the younger prisoners, including Arnold, slept on the floor.

At five the next morning, when the prisoners were awakened, they discovered that their shoes, so neatly arranged the evening before, had been jumbled together into a large pile by the guards.

Blum ended up with a pair of mismatched shoes, much too small for his large feet.

This first full day was strictly for the prisoners to be processed; no meals were provided. Over the course of the day, the prisoners were photographed, fingerprinted, assigned an identification number, shorn of their hair, hosed down in the shower room, examined medically, and given ill-fitting clothes. Once inside their permanent barrack, the *kapo* (the prisoner in charge of the barrack) then gave each man a spoon to eat with, but each prisoner had to share an aluminum pan with one other prisoner for their meals.

Then the kapo taught the prisoners about the camp rules:

We would be marched to the drill field every morning and evening to be counted. There would be no food until the count was accepted by the SS. In the unlikely event of an escape, no prisoner could eat until the escapee was caught and returned. Anyone dying during the day or night had to be carried to the drill field for the count. . . . Our names were not to be used. Instead we were to refer to ourselves as *Schutzhaftjude*, Jew in Protective Custody, and our camp number.[7]

Besides Dachau, Jewish men and boys were also sent to concentration camps at Sachsenhausen and Buchenwald. The brutal treatment of the Jewish detainees was similar in all three camps.

A rabbi named Dr. Georg Wilde described his introduction to Buchenwald:

> We stood on our feet from morning until evening to be trained in camp "discipline." Three men were flogged twenty-five times each. . . . When the victims cried out they received twenty-five more blows. . . . I realized that they were trying to unnerve us, to sap our wills and our dignity. An SS officer began screaming, "None of you will leave this camp alive." And from that moment I vowed no matter the cost and no matter how brutal the spectacle I was made to endure, I would not allow my will or my dignity to be belittled.[8]

A reporter for a London newspaper wrote about the fate of sixty-two Jewish men who had been sent to Sachsenhausen after Kristallnacht. Escorted by German police, they were turned over to SS guards at the concentration camp. The men were forced to run between two rows of SS guards who beat them with shovels, clubs, and whips. The men fell and were beaten further. When they had finished, "twelve of the sixty-two were dead, their skulls smashed. The others were all unconscious. The eyes of some had been knocked out, their faces flattened and shapeless."[9]

The Sandwich

After about two and a half weeks, Arnold was unexpectedly released. He had gotten used to the daily routine as best as he could, even the terrible meals that were served at lunch and dinner. Lunch especially was a difficult meal at the camp because it usually included pork-blood sausage, which violated his strict religious dietary laws. Judaism prohibits the eating of pork and any type of blood.

When Arnold Blum arrived at Dachau, all the prisoners' shoes were taken away and thrown in a large pile. Blum had to wear shoes that were too small for him. This huge pile of victims' shoes was discovered at Dachau after the camp was liberated in 1945.

Still, in order to survive, Arnold ate the sausage every day it was provided. As he recalled later, eating the sausage "had been my first exposure to non-kosher food and I had gagged as it crossed my lips. Eating had posed a moral dilemma to me, whether to starve or live in violation of religious law."[10]

On the day of his release from Dachau, the man accompanying Arnold bought two sandwiches for the journey at the Munich train station and gave one to Blum. Excited by the prospect of real food after their imprisonment, both men unwrapped the sandwiches and began to eat them.

A rabbi who had also been released from Dachau was sitting in their train compartment and observed that the two men were eating ham sandwiches. He scolded them, "the Holy One . . . just liberated you from that terrible place and in gratitude the first

Inmates doing forced labor at the Dachau concentration camp.

thing you do is to eat pork. You ought to be terribly ashamed of yourselves."[11]

Blum rode to Stuttgart in silence, confused about the dilemma he faced. "In the choice between starvation and living in violation of religious law," he wrote later, "I had opted for life. Was it worse to eat ham now? I didn't know."[12]

A Violent Confrontation

In April 1939, Arnold emigrated to the United States. As soon as he could, he joined the United States Army. By the end of World War II, he was a private first class in an infantry division. After the war, his unit remained in Germany to help with postwar relations.

One day, a local resident informed Arnold that a Nazi who had actively participated in Kristallnacht still lived in the area. Not only that, but the man—named Herr Schluemper—had boasted about participating in Kristallnacht by beating Jews and stealing their property afterward. Although all citizens were supposed to have been questioned by British authorities to weed out any Nazi sympathizers, Schluemper had escaped notice.

Though not part of his duties and clearly against military rules, Arnold decided that he had to deal with Schluemper.

One night, he drove to Herr Schluemper's house and rang the doorbell. When Schluemper's teenage daughter answered, Arnold told her he wished to discuss a personal matter with her father.

In a few moments, Schluemper finally stood in front of him. Arnold told him, "I've made extensive inquiries about you. . . .

A Russian survivor, liberated by the U.S. Army at the Buchenwald camp in Germany, identifies a former camp guard who brutally beat prisoners. Most Holocaust victims did not have an opportunity for revenge, but Arnold Blum took his chance after the war.

You participated in the beating of Jews and the destruction of their property in Bremen during the night of [November 9 and 10, 1938], and you even bragged about it."[13]

Although Schluemper denied the charges, Arnold, unable to contain himself any longer, relived the anger he felt on Kristallnacht in Stuttgart. He called the man a liar and

> let fly a tremendous haymaker which landed on his nose. He raised his arms to defend himself, but I caught him under the chin with a left uppercut which straightened him. Then I hit him again, even harder than the first time, and caught him on his left temple, knocking him down. His head hit the concrete floor with a thud and he lay at my feet motionless. I was tempted to kick his head, but did not.[14]

Blum walked away from the house and climbed into the car. He had achieved something that most victims of the Nazis never did: an opportunity for revenge.

After the war, he returned to the United States and became an engineer. Today, he lives with his wife near Pittsburgh, Pennsylvania.

9   Alfred Werner

On the morning of November 10, as Alfred Werner walked to his friend Jacob's house in the center of Vienna, Austria, he was unaware of the November pogrom. At a neighborhood newsstand, he paused to browse the morning headlines. The newspaper, now controlled by the Nazis, announced the death of Ernst vom Rath with blatant antisemitic headlines.

That morning, Alfred wondered how this news would affect him as an Austrian Jew. Life in Vienna had grown difficult for Jews once Hitler had annexed Austria, creating a forced *Anschluss* (a union). Almost immediately, Jews had been harassed, robbed, physically abused, and sometimes killed. Many had their businesses and apartments taken away from them.

Realizing that the death of vom Rath might start a new wave of antisemitism, Alfred decided to return home. He hurried to a nearby phone booth to let Jacob know that he would not be visiting that day.

Jacob's wife answered with alarming news. Her husband had gone to the grocery store two hours earlier and had not returned. Alfred tried to comfort her, but he was interrupted by an angry man who told him to get off the phone.

Austrian citizens in Vienna celebrate the arrival of German troops into the city after the Anschluss. While some Austrians celebrated, many did not, and most Jews, including Alfred Werner, found life increasingly difficult.

AUSTRIAN JEWS UNDER THE ANSCHLUSS

Many Jews in Austria were brutalized after the Anschluss, and life became unbearable. In this photo, a group of Jews wait in line to receive exit visas in Vienna with hopes of fleeing the country.

On March 12, 1938, German troops marched into Austria, effectively joining it with Germany in an Anschluss. With this forced annexation, Germany also inherited two hundred thousand Austrian Jews, most of whom lived in Vienna. To achieve their goal of a *Judenfrei* country, Nazi terror tactics were used against the Austrian Jews.

During the first few weeks of the Anschluss, Austrian Jews were the victims of more outrageous and unbelievable cruelty than German Jews had been during the last five years.[1] On April 23, 1938, for example, a Saturday and the day of Sabbath for Jews, a number of elderly Jews were rounded up in Vienna by SS troops and trucked to the Prater Amusement Park, where they were brutalized with a variety of "pleasure hours."[2] When the SS gave the command, the victims, which included pregnant women,

> . . . had to run in circles until they fainted and collapsed. Those pretending to have fainted in order to escape the ordeal were beaten until they got up and ran again. . . . Another favorite torture was the famous scenic railway in the Prater amusement park, where large number of Jews were forced into the carries, tied to their seats, and then driven at top speed until they lost consciousness. . . . Hundreds of Jewish people were taken to the hospital during the following days with severe heart attacks, and in no few cases these "pleasure hours" brought about heart-failure and death.[3]

As the Austria-Germany union progressed, many Austrian Jews committed suicide. During the first two months of the Anschluss, between 1,500 and 2,000 people committed suicide, primarily in Vienna.[4]

Alfred politely told the man that he would have to wait until he completed his call. As Alfred exited the booth a short time later, he noticed that the man wore a swastika badge announcing his membership in the Nazi Party. Alfred quickly headed home.

Arrested and Detained

Before he could reach his apartment, he was accosted on the street by another man who asked if he was a Jew. Alfred eyed the man and wondered if he was a robber. "The man who asked me this question had the look of a criminal; he wore no badge. Frequently Jews were robbed in the streets in Nazi Vienna in broad daylight. So intimidated were the Jews that they often did not dare call for help."[5]

Alfred hurried away but the man confronted him again. Other people on the street, most of them wearing Nazi badges, noticed the trouble and stopped as well.

"Let him alone, at once!" some of the people told the troublemaker.[6]

Alfred realized that even though they wore Nazi Party badges, they were only trying to protect themselves; they were not truly Nazi Party members.

But the assailant pulled a badge out of his coat to warn the assembled crowd that he was a Gestapo agent. The people quickly dispersed, and Alfred was placed in handcuffs. Then he was "dragged like a common criminal through the crowded streets . . . on that gloomy November day" to a holding cell in a police station.[7]

After his arrest, Alfred Werner did not know that synagogues, homes, and businesses were being destroyed in Vienna. This young man in Munich, Germany, carries a large Star of David that has been removed from a synagogue that was in fiery ruins.

Tortured by Nazis

Alfred shared the cell with some fifty or sixty other Jews at first. They had been arrested on the street or taken from their stores or homes. "Our number increased as every five or ten minutes," Alfred wrote in 1958 when he recounted his experience for a magazine, "another battered Jew was thrown into our already crowded cell."[8]

According to Alfred, neither he nor his companions knew that synagogues were being burned or that shops were being ransacked and destroyed. Their police guards did not share any information with them.

That night, Nazi storm troopers came to cart them away. They were pushed into a police van and driven to their SA barracks, housed in a former school:

> On our arrival we had to run the gauntlet of a wild mob who beat us with sticks and iron bars. The first [man] to enter the barracks was shot at once. On entering the hall, he had stumbled against a Nazi guard, and another Nazi, interpreting it as a hostile act, had pressed the trigger.[9]

The men spent the night wondering what would happen to them next and whether they would ever see their families again. The unknown was unbearable for some.

> *Three or four persons went mad that night.*
> *A boy of eighteen tried to commit suicide*
> *by jumping out the window. As his head*
> *smashed through the glass he was seized*
> *and pulled back by one of our men. . . .*
> *The man was too late. The boy had cut*
> *one of the arteries of his neck and he died*
> *despite the frantic efforts of some doctors*
> *in our midst.*[10]

A Week With the Devil

The men spent a week in the barracks, surviving only on small
quantities of bread and tea. During that time the guards "played
with us as nasty boys would play with their 'pets.'"[11]

One guard, described by Alfred as a devil, told the men to
choose one man who would pay "for the sins of the others."[12]
When the men refused, the guard picked a prisoner and took him
from the room. Alfred never saw him again.

On another day, a guard confronted a seventeen-year-old
boy—the youngest person in the group—by putting a gun to
the boy's chest. When the guard demanded that the boy recite
his prayers, the boy defiantly told him, "Shoot, you coward!"[13]
This angered the guard so much that he beat the boy with his
gun until he fell to the floor.

On their last night in the barracks, they were sent into the
schoolhouse gym where they were lectured by one guard. He told

them, "You have murdered Herr vom Rath. . . . Every one of you is a Herschel Grynszpan. But our Führer will destroy Jewry in all parts of the world, and not even your Jehovah will help you!"[14]

They were forced to exercise next, from ten o'clock that night until eight the next morning:

> We had to run, jump, kneel without pause. Not only the young strong men, but also the elderly and the sick had to keep up pace. . . . Several men collapsed. The Nazis "took charge" of these "recalcitrant" ones in such a way that in the morning two or three were found dead.[15]

The next morning the guards told them that they would report to the office where they would learn what would happen next. Alfred and the other men hoped that they would be able to return home to see their families and make arrangements to emigrate.

But their hopes were dashed when they were pushed into cattle cars and transported to Dachau.

Christmas at Dachau

At Dachau, Alfred was placed in a group of some 800 men and given prisoner number 27,660.[16] Most of the prisoners were Jewish and had been arrested during Kristallnacht, but others were Gentiles (Christians) jailed for their political beliefs.

After spending a week in prison barracks in Vienna, Alfred Werner learned that he was being deported to Dachau. Gustav Straus, after his arrest during Kristallnacht, wrote this postcard to his wife and son in Essen, Germany, en route to imprisonment at Dachau.

A week before Christmas 1938, the camp commandant erected a fifteen-foot-tall Christmas tree in the central parade yard. Alfred found this odd because the Nazis professed their strong opposition to religion. Every night, after being drilled on the parade grounds, the prisoners

were forced to stand at attention for two or three hours at a stretch, to contemplate the Christmas tree, most of us . . . too weak and too frozen to enjoy [its] beauties. . . . Storm troopers silently moved throughout

> *rows, cycling through the deep snow, ready to strike if a man dared to turn his head away.*[17]

Alfred had heard that the Jews would be released soon. On December 22, the group was ordered to remove all the snow and ice from the camp immediately. Using wheelbarrows, the men had to move quickly or they would be kicked by roving storm troopers. Alfred saw "an elderly man whose loaded wheelbarrow skidded into the water where we had to dump the snow. The Nazi guard kicked him into the icy water, too."[18] His body was not moved until after Christmas.

Release and Emigration

After a few months at Dachau, Alfred's visa for the United States was approved. He was released from Dachau and left Germany right away. He became a well-respected art historian, but he also wrote about his memory of Kristallnacht and his time at Dachau.

Albert Fuchs had practiced law in Karlsruhe, Germany, for twenty years when the Nazis began to strip the rights of Jews. Still, as a veteran of World War I, who had received the Iron Cross for bravery as an officer, he considered himself a German patriot; he wore his war medals every day as a symbol of how much he loved his country. He hoped the new antisemitic laws and decrees would disappear in a few years and that his four children would be able to live without fear. As a lawyer, he was also able to help many Jews as their rights were taken away by the Nazis.

Near the end of September 1938, however, a new law prevented Albert from practicing law. Even with this setback, he and his wife, who was not Jewish, tried to maintain a safe haven for their children. Albert believed that he and his family "possessed the spiritual and physical strength to survive" the Nazi rule in Germany.[1]

A photo of Albert Fuchs taken before Kristallnacht in 1938.

Kristallnacht

Everything changed when the news of Ernst vom Rath's death was announced on the evening of November 9:

> Late that night, the radio broadcast the decree of the SS Reichsführer Heinrich Himmler: that unless all Jews turned in their firearms, they would be placed in "protective custody" for a minimum of twenty years. We went to bed filled with apprehension.[2]

The first phone call rang at three o'clock on the morning of November 10. An unknown male caller warned the family that they should be "most careful."[3] Albert and his wife were not sure what to do, since they felt safe in their home. They could not go back to sleep, but they listened alertly to any sounds outside.

A second call at four-thirty that morning came from another unknown male speaking from a pay phone. The voice told his wife, "Why don't you quickly lead your husband to safety?"[4]

Albert considered driving off but decided not to do anything hasty, because he did not know what awaited him outside in their still-quiet neighborhood. He and his wife listened to the radio but did not hear any reports about an action against Jews. Finally, they chose to do nothing out of the ordinary. He did not want to upset his mother, who lived with them, or his children, who were getting ready for school.

Albert Fuchs received the Iron Cross for bravery as an officer during World War I.

News of Kristallnacht

The first outside news came with the arrival of his assistant, who reported that a local bank owned by a Jew had been destroyed during the night. Then they learned that the synagogue and Jewish school had been set ablaze and their contents thrown into the streets. Next, his wife heard what had happened at a hotel where fifty Jews were living while waiting for permission to emigrate. A Nazi mob "went from room to room, systematically destroying the furnishings, slashing the bedding, and hacking the furniture to pieces. The residents were kicked and beaten and all the men taken into custody in a brutal manner."[5]

By mid-morning, the news of Kristallnacht became much more personal. Albert discovered that his cousin had committed suicide. Then he learned that other friends had been arrested.

A view of a Jewish-owned shop in Berlin completely destroyed during Kristallnacht. The Fuchs family witnessed the violence and damage done in their town of Karlsruhe.

Albert's wife pleaded with him to leave town as soon as possible. He quickly packed and headed for their weekend house, driving out of town by back roads.

A Change of Mind

Their weekend house was quite rustic and had little food in the cupboard when he arrived, but Albert was afraid to go into the nearby village and shop for groceries. Because his wife was Aryan, she could travel freely. She and one of their sons drove to the house and brought food and news of everything that had occurred. She described what had happened to the Jewish men and boys who had been taken away during Kristallnacht; they had been taken to Dachau. Albert and his wife decided to use two of their sons as messengers from then on.

The grim events of Kristallnacht changed Albert's mind about staying in Germany. When he heard "that mixed marriages were to be annulled and the children of such marriages handed over to the State," he and his wife decided that they would rather be "beggars in a foreign country" with their children.[6]

Still, when someone advised him to flee Germany at once, without his wife or children, Albert hesitated. Even though he was ready to leave, he was not prepared to go without his family.

Jewish men arrested during Kristallnacht line up for roll call at the Buchenwald concentration camp in November 1938. In order to avoid arrest, Albert Fuchs fled the country.

Crossing the Border

A friend warned the family that they should be very careful on Sunday, November 13, the day of Ernst vom Rath's funeral. After that was over, they were told to waste no time in leaving. Albert was fortunate, in that he had a valid German passport with a French visa. This meant that he could travel to France whenever he pleased. Because his wife and children did not have such passports, he would have to leave first while his family obtained visas.

Early on the morning of November 14, Albert drove back to his home in Karlsruhe and parked some blocks away. He stole

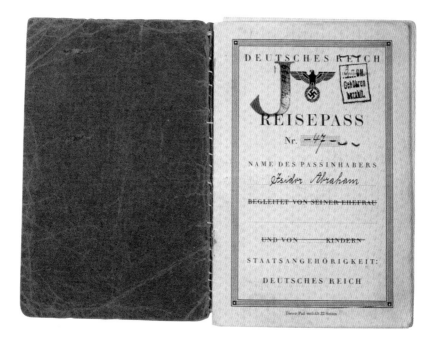

Because Albert Fuchs had a valid passport and a French visa, he escaped to France. Like all German Jews, Fuchs's passport was stamped wth a red "J" as required by Nazi law.

into his house in darkness and hid all day. During that time, he prepared the papers to dissolve his legal practice. The next day, he packed a small briefcase and left for the border town of Kehl.

At first, the border police regarded him as an emigrant and refused to let him pass. His passport and other papers, however, finally reassured them that he had the authority to travel to France. When he insisted that he had a business meeting in Strasbourg, they let him pass. He made his way to the train to Strasbourg, where another Jewish man joined him in his compartment:

> His hand luggage was in shreds and he himself was in ghastly shape. The left side of his face was an unrecognizable black and blue mess. He must have been punched or kicked in the face. We exchanged a silent glance. Before I could give him a word of comfort, he rushed into another compartment where acquaintances were waiting for him. Then the train went slowly across the Rhine Bridge.[7]

As the train crossed the bridge into France, Albert opened the window beside him. Then he took the medals that he had been awarded for his bravery fighting for Germany in World War I and threw them into the water below.

A New Life

During the rest of his train ride to Strasbourg, Albert wrote an account of what the last week had been like for him, his family and relatives, and the Jews of Germany. He was able to reunite with his family. Eventually, they moved to Canada, where he became a practicing lawyer, too.

Before he died in 1972, he made sure that his written record of Kristallnacht was part of a university archive that contained the unpublished diaries and journals of Holocaust survivors.

KRISTALLNACHT: A MISLEADING NAME

The pogrom that occurred from November 7–10 did not have an official name; the term *Kristallnacht* came sometime later. No one knows who invented the term, but it is a *euphemism* (a pleasant-sounding word used to conceal a harsh truth or reality).

Many historians and Holocaust educators find the word misleading for at least two reasons. First, it suggests that the violence lasted only one night, when it was actually spread over a four-day period. Second, "the night of broken glass" emphasizes the destruction of property rather than the violence (beatings, incarceration, and murder) directed at Germany's Jews.

In Germany today, many people refer to *Kristallnacht* with two other names: *Novemberpogrome* (the November pogrom) and the *Reichspogromnacht* (the government pogrom night).[8]

No matter what the events of November 7–10 are called, the pogrom was a clear message to all remaining German Jews: they could no longer wait to leave the country. More than two hundred thousand Jews fled before the next year was out.[9]

With the beginning of World War II in September 1939, all Jews who remained in Germany and Austria—and those in European countries eventually invaded by the Nazis—were caught in the terror of the Holocaust.

Kristallnacht had been the clear and vivid signal of Nazi intentions. It was, as historian Martin Gilbert wrote, "a brutal . . . uninhibited assault on everything Jewish."[10]

1933

January 30—Adolf Hitler appointed chancellor of Germany by Paul von Hindenburg.

April 1—One-day boycott of Jewish shops, doctors, and lawyers.

April 7—Restoration of the Professional Civil Services Act enacted to prohibit non-Aryans working in civil service jobs.

May 10—Joseph Goebbels and the Nazi German Student Association coordinate the burning of "un-German" books.

July 14—The Nazi Party declared the only legal political party in Germany.

September 29—Jews prohibited from owning farmland. Jews who worked in film, theater, music, and the fine arts prohibited from working.

1934

January 1—Jewish holidays removed from government calendar.

1935

May 21—Army Law enacted to make Jews ineligible for military service.

September 15—Nuremberg Laws, known as Laws for the Protection of German Blood and German Honor, enacted.

November 14—A new decree defines a Jew as anyone with two Jewish grandparents (even if they had converted to Christianity) and includes anyone considered *mischlinge* (that is, part Jewish, such as a person with only one Jewish parent).

1936

March 7—Jews prohibited from voting in parliamentary elections.

1937

Spring—Jews prohibited from owning businesses in Germany.

April 11—German Interior Registry issues decree revoking the citizenship of Jews.

1938

April 24—Decree Concerning the Reporting of Jewish Property enacted to require Jews to register all the real estate they owned with the government.

July 21—Jews required to apply for special identity cards.

July 25—A new regulation requires Jewish doctors to treat only Jewish patients.

July 27—Jewish street names in Germany changed to German names.

September 27—Jewish lawyers prohibited from practicing.

October 5—Passports of Jews recalled to be reissued and marked with a "J" for *Jude*.

October 28—Herschel Grynszpan's family expelled from Germany along with 17,000 other Polish Jews.

November 7—Herschel Grynszpan murders Ernst vom Rath. Local riots against Jews begin in and around Kassel.

November 8—Jewish newspapers and magazines prohibited from further publication; Jewish children prohibited from attending German elementary schools. Local riots spread to Hesse.

November 9—Ernst vom Rath dies; Joseph Goebbels initiates Kristallnacht in Germany and Austria.

November 10—Kristallnacht pogrom in Germany and Austria.

November 11—Jews prohibited from owning firearms.

November 12—Decree on the Elimination of the Jews from German Economic Life prohibits Jews from operating stores, sales agencies, and from carrying on a trade. Jews fined one billion marks to pay for damages caused by Kristallnacht.

November 15—Jewish children prohibited from attending German schools and are only allowed to attend Jewish schools.

December 3—Decree Concerning the Use of Jewish Property forced Jews to close their businesses or sell them at highly reduced prices to "Aryans."

1939

September 1—Germany invades Poland; World War II begins.

October 19—Fine against Jews for damages caused on Kristallnacht raised to 1.25 billion marks.

1940

May 13—Germany invades France.

1941

January 18—Herschel Grynszpan sent to Sachsenhausen.

October 30—Grynszpan indicted for murder of Ernst vom Rath.

1942

February–May—Date for trial of Herschel Grynszpan scheduled twice and postponed.

September 26—Herschel Grynszpan reportedly transferred to Magdeburg, a sub-camp of Buchenwald.

1960

June 1—Grynszpan declared dead by West German government.

Chapter Notes

Introduction

1. Francis H. Schott, "Kristallnacht, in Solingen," *New York Times,* November 9, 1988, p. A35.
2. Ibid.
3. Mitchell G. Bard, *48 Hours of Kristallnacht: Night of Destruction/Dawn of the Holocaust* (Guilford, Conn.: The Lyons Press, 2008), p. 1.
4. Ronnie S. Landau, *The Nazi Holocaust* (Chicago: Ivan R. Dee, 2006), p. 123.
5. Martin Gilbert, *Kristallnacht: Prelude to Destruction* (New York: Harper Perennial, 2007), p. 131.
6. Anthony Read and David Fisher, *Kristallnacht: The Unleashing of the Holocaust* (New York: Peter Bedrick Books, 1989), p. 49.
7. Alan E. Steinweis, *Kristallnacht 1938* (Cambridge, Mass.: The Belknap Press of Harvard University Press, 2009), p. 19.
8. Ibid., p. 21.
9. Ibid., p. 6.
10. Ibid., p. 24.
11. Read and Fisher, p. 61.
12. Steinweis, p. 29.
13. Gerald Schwab, *The Day the Holocaust Began: The Odyssey of Herschel Grynszpan* (New York: Praeger, 1990), p. 21.
14. Norman Bentwich, "Kristallnacht: Pogrom in Emden," in Azriel Eisenberg, *Witness to the Holocaust* (New York: Pilgrim Press, 1981), p. 84.
15. "Dispatches From American Diplomats," in *Night of Pogroms: "Kristallnacht" November 9–10, 1938* (Washington, D.C.: U.S. Holocaust Memorial Council, no date), p. 34.
16. Steinweis, p. 8.
17. Anthony Read, *The Devil's Disciples: Hitler's Inner Circle* (New York: W. W. Norton & Company, 2005), p. 515.
18. Steinweis, p. 73.
19. Ibid., p. 107.
20. Gilbert, p. 183.
21. Ibid., p. 144.
22. Landau, p. 144.
23. Ibid., p. 147.
24. Ibid.

Chapter 1. **Herschel Grynszpan**

1. Gerald Schwab, *The Day the Holocaust Began: The Odyssey of Herschel Grynszpan* (New York: Praeger, 1990), p. 4.
2. Ibid., p. 44.
3. Andy Marino, *Herschel: The Boy Who Started World War II* (Boston: Faber and Faber, 1995), p. 41.
4. Schwab, p. 55.
5. Marino, p. 63.
6. Schwab, p. 74.
7. Ibid., pp. 74–75.
8. Marino, p. 84.
9. Rita Thalmann and Emmanuel Feinermann, *Crystal Night: 9–10 November 1938* (New York: Coward, McCann, & Geoghegan, 1974), p. 48.
10. Marino, p. 199.
11. Anthony Read and David Fisher, *Kristallnacht: The Unleashing of the Holocaust* (New York: Peter Bedrick Books, 1989), p. 255.
12. James Ardolin and Norbert Brenner, "Zbaszyn: Deportation to the Border Town Camp—1938," Holocaust Research Project, 2008, <http://www.holocaustresearchproject.org/holoprelude/Zbaszyn.html> (April 9, 2010).
13. Schwab, p. 102.

Chapter 2. **Joseph Goebbels**

1. Roger Manvell and Heinrich Fraenkel, *Doctor Goebbels: His Life and Death* (London: Greenhill Books, 2006), p. 18.
2. Ibid., p. 49.
3. Ibid., p. 59.
4. Ibid., pp. 61–62.
5. Ibid., p. 69.
6. Ibid., p. 130.
7. Sir Nevile Henderson, *Failure of a Mission* (New York: G. P. Putnam's Sons, 1940), pp. 71–72.
8. Ian Kershaw, *Hitler: A Biography* (New York: W. W. Norton & Company, 2008), p. 457.
9. Anthony Read, *The Devil's Disciples: Hitler's Inner Circle* (New York: W. W. Norton & Company, 2005), p. 510.
10. "Joseph Goebbels on Kristallnacht: From the Diary of Joseph

Goebbels," Yad Vashem History of the Holocaust, n.d., <http://www.zupdom.com/icons-multimedia/ClientsArea/HoH/LIBARC/ARCHIVE/Chapters/Terror/Kristall/GoebbelK.html> (August 19, 2009).
11. "Gestapo Orders on Kristallnact, November 9–20, 1938," The History Place, World War II in Europe, n.d., <http://www.historyplace.com/worldwar2/timeline/knacht1a.htm> (October 4, 2009).
12. Ibid.
13. Rita Thalmann and Emmanuel Feinermann, *Crystal Night: 9–10 November 1938* (New York: Coward, McCann, & Geoghegan, 1974), p. 89.

Chapter 3. Hannele Zürndorfer

1. Hannele Zürndorfer, *The Ninth of November* (London: Quartet Books, reprint edition, 1989), p. 31.
2. Ibid., p. 46.
3. Ibid.
4. Ibid., p. 48.
5. Ibid., p. 50.
6. Ibid.
7. Ibid., pp. 58–59.
8. Ibid., pp. 60–61.
9. Ibid., p. 62.
10. Ibid.
11. Ibid., pp. 62–63.
12. Ibid., p. 64.
13. Ibid., p. 67.

Chapter 4. Fred Spiegel

1. Fred Spiegel, *Once the Acacias Bloomed* (Margate, N.J.: ComteQ Publishing, 2004), p. 24.
2. Ibid., p. 26.
3. Ibid., pp. 26–27.
4. Ibid., pp. 27–28.
5. "Bette and Joseph Seligmann," Familie Aron Oppenheimer, December 27, 2007, <http://wp.ge-mittelkreis.de/webfric05/webinsch/jupage/foppen6.htm> (September 29, 2009).
6. Spiegel, pp. 76–77.
7. Ibid., p. 77.
8. Ibid.
9. Ibid., pp. 87–88.
10. Ibid., p. 101.

11. Ibid., p. 158.

Chapter 5. Ernest Fontheim

1. Ernest Günter Fontheim, United States Holocaust Memorial Museum (USHMM), Oral History Interview, March 13, 1997, RG-50.030*0450.
2. Ibid.
3. Ibid.
4. Anthony Read and David Fisher, *Kristallnacht: The Unleashing of the Holocaust* (New York: Peter Bedrick Books, 1989), p. 98.
5. Saul Friedlander, *Nazi Germany and the Jews, Volume I, The Years of Persecution* (New York: Harper Perennial, 1998), p. 276.
6. Read and Fisher, p. 180.
7. Ulrich Klug, "Permission for Murder," in Jörg Wollenberg, ed., *The German Public and the Persecution of the Jews 1933–1945*, trans. and ed. Rado Pribic (Atlantic Highlands, N.J.: Humanities Press, 1996), pp. 66–67.
8. Fontheim.
9. Ibid.

Chapter 6. Marianne Strauss

1. Mark Roseman, *A Past in Hiding: Memory and Survival in Nazi Germany* (New York: Metropolitan Books, 2001), p. 51.
2. Ibid., p. 70.
3. Ibid., p. 74.
4. Ibid.
5. Ibid., p. 126.
6. Ibid., p. 127.
7. Ibid., p. 128.
8. Ibid., p. 2.
9. Ibid., p. 269.
10. Ibid., p. 3.
11. Ibid., p. 290.
12. Ibid., p. 419.

Chapter 7. Jurgen Herbst

1. Jurgen Herbst, *Requiem for a German Past* (Madison: University of Wisconsin Press, 1999), p. 12.
2. Ibid., p. 69.
3. Ibid., p. 70.
4. Ibid.
5. Ibid.

6. Ibid.
7. "Kristallnacht+70: Night of Broken Glass," *Simon Wiesenthal Center*, 2008, <http://www.wiesenthal.com/atf/cf/%7BDFD2AAC1-2ADE-428A-9263-35234229D8D8%7D/KRISTALLNACHT.PDF> (February 12, 2010).
8. Ibid.
9. Ibid.
10. Herbst, p. 73.
11. Ibid.
12. Ibid., p. 74.
13. Ibid., p. 75.
14. Ibid., p. 76.
15. Ibid., p. 77.
16. Ibid., pp. 77–78.
17. Ibid., p. 169.
18. Ibid., p. 171.
19. Ibid., p. 223.

Chapter 8. Arnold Blum

1. Samuel Honaker, "American Consul Samuel Honaker's Description of Anti-Semitic Persecution and *Kristallnacht* and Its Aftereffects in the Stuttgart Region (November 12 and November 15, 1938)," GHDI (German History in Documents and Images), n.d., <http://germanhistorydocs.ghi-dc.org/sub_document.cfm?document_id=1525> (August 21, 2009).
2. Arnold Blum, "An Action Against the Jews," in Anita Brostoff with Sheila Chamovitz, eds., *Flares of Memory: Stories of Childhood During the Holocaust* (New York: Oxford University Press, 1998), p. 20.
3. Honacker.
4. Blum, p. 22.
5. Rita Thalmann and Emmanuel Feinermann, *Crystal Night: 9–10 November 1938* (New York: Coward, McCann, & Geoghegan, 1974), p. 117.
6. Arnold Blum, "Dachau," in Anita Brostoff with Sheila Chamovitz, eds., *Flares of Memory: Stories of Childhood During the Holocaust* (New York: Oxford University Press, 1998), p. 50.
7. Ibid., p. 53.
8. Thalmann and Feinermann, p. 129.
9. Martin Gilbert, *Kristallnacht: Prelude to Destruction* (New York: Harper Perennial, 2007), p. 167.
10. Blum, p. 22.
11. Ibid., p. 23.
12. Ibid.

13. Arnold Blum, "Herr Schluemper," in Anita Brostoff with Sheila Chamovitz, eds., *Flares of Memory: Stories of Childhood During the Holocaust* (New York: Oxford University Press, 1998), p. 271.
14. Ibid.

Chapter 9. **Alfred Werner**

1. Rita Thalmann and Emmanuel Feinermann, *Crystal Night: 9–10 November 1938* (New York: Coward, McCann, & Geoghegan, 1974), p. 15.
2. Oswald Dutch, *Thus Died Austria* (London: Edward Arnold, 1938), p. 246.
3. Ibid., 247.
4. Ibid., p. 248.
5. Alfred Werner, "Terror in Vienna," in Azriel Eisenberg, ed., *Witness to the Holocaust* (New York: Pilgrim Press, 1981), p. 88.
6. Ibid.
7. Ibid., p. 89.
8. Ibid.
9. Ibid.
10. Ibid.
11. Ibid., p. 90.
12. Ibid.
13. Ibid.
14. Ibid.
15. Ibid.
16. Harold Marcuse, *Legacies of Dachau: The Uses and Abuses of Concentration Camps, 1933–2001* (New York: Cambridge University Press, 2001), p. 173.
17. Alfred Werner, "Christmas in Dachau," in Patrick Jordan and Paul Baumann, eds., *Commonweal Confronts the Century: Liberal Convictions, Catholic Tradition* (New York: Touchstone, 1999), p. 196.
18. Ibid.

Chapter 10. **Albert Fuchs**

1. "Albert Fuchs: My Experience From November 9th Through 16th 1938," Montreal Institute for Genocide and Human Rights Studies (MIGS), n.d., <http://migs.concordia.ca/memoirs/fuchs_albert/fuchs_albert_01.htm> (September 30, 2009).
2. Ibid.
3. Ibid.
4. Ibid.
5. Ibid.

6. Ibid.
7. Ibid.
8. Alan E. Steinweis, *Kristallnacht 1938* (Cambridge, Mass.: The Belknap Press of Harvard University Press, 2009), p. 2.
9. Mitchell G. Bard, *48 Hours of Kristallnacht: Night of Destruction/Dawn of the Holocaust* (Guilford, Conn.: The Lyons Press, 2008), p. 200.
10. Martin Gilbert, *Kristallnacht: Prelude to Destruction* (New York: Harper Perennial, 2007), p. 269.

Permissions

Fred Spiegel & ComteQ Publishing, Margate, N.J.

Excerpt from *A Past in Hiding: Memory and Survival in Nazi Germany* by Mark Roseman. Copyright © 2001 by Mark Roseman. Reprinted by arrangement with Henry Holt and Company, LLC.

Herbst, Jurgen. *Requiem for a German Past.* © 1999 by the Board of Regents of the University of Wisconsin System. Reprinted by permission of The University of Wisconsin Press.

By permission of Oxford University Press, Inc. *Flares of Memory: Stories of Childhood During the Holocaust* edited by Anita Brostoff with Sheila Chamovitz.

Glossary

Bund Deutscher Mädel—League of German Girls (abbreviated BDM), the female component of the Hitler Youth movement.

cantor—The official of a synagogue who sings or chants the prayers.

emigrate—To leave one country and settle in another.

Gestapo—The Nazi political police, a secret organization.

kapo—Prisoner in charge of a concentration camp barrack who was responsible for carrying out Nazi orders.

Kindertransport—Literally, the "children's transport," an organized effort that saved ten thousand Jewish children in Europe from the Holocaust by bringing them to safety in England.

pogrom—A brutal and violent action usually aimed at a particular ethnic or religious group.

quota—A prescribed or limited number. In 1938, the United States had certain immigration quotas, limiting the number of a people who could enter the country legally.

rabbi—The main religious leader of a synagogue.

SA—Short for *Sturmabteilung*, or storm troopers, in German, a part of the Nazi party that wore brown shirts and promoted violence against Jews; important participants in Kristallnacht.

SS—Short for *Schutzstaffel*, or "Protective Squadron" in German, a police and military organization that was highly loyal to Adolf Hitler. Among other duties, the SS supervised the concentration camps. As a result, the SS was responsible for most of the war crimes committed by Germany during World War II.

yeshiva—A school where students study sacred Jewish texts.

Further Reading

Books

Bartoletti, Susan Campbell. *Hitler Youth: Growing Up in Hitler's Shadow*. New York: Scholastic Nonfiction, 2005.

Fitzgerald, Stephanie. *Kristallnacht, the Night of Broken Glass: Igniting the Nazi War Against Jews*. Minneapolis, Minn.: Compass Point Books, 2008.

Lee, Carol Ann. *Anne Frank and the Children of the Holocaust*. New York: Puffin, 2008.

Mara, Wil. *Kristallnacht: Nazi Persecution of the Jews in Europe*. New York: Marshall Cavendish Benchmark, 2009.

Zullo, Allan and Mara Bovsun. *Survivors: True Stories of Children in the Holocaust*. New York: Scholastic, 2004.

Internet Addresses

It Came From Within . . . 71 Years Since Kristallnacht: Yad Vashem

<http://www1.yadvashem.org/exhibitions/kristallnacht/index.html>

Kristallnacht: Night of Broken Glass

<http://www.holocaustandhumanity.org/kristallnacht/index.html>

The United States Holocaust Memorial Museum—Kristallnacht: The November 1938 Pogroms

<http://www.ushmm.org/museum/exhibit/online/kristallnacht/frame.htm>

Index